RUTH

Ruth

A Migrant's Tale

ILANA PARDES

Yale

UNIVERSITY

PRESS

New Haven and London

Yale University Press books may be purchased in quantity for educational, business, or promotional use. For information, please e-mail sales.press@yale.edu (U.S. office) or sales@yaleup.co.uk (U.K. office).

Set in Janson Oldstyle type by Integrated Publishing Solutions.
Printed in the United States of America.

Library of Congress Control Number: 2021950218
ISBN 978-0-300-25507-2 (hardcover : alk. paper)

A catalogue record for this book is available from the British Library.

This paper meets the requirements of ANSI/NISO Z39.48-1992
(Permanence of Paper).

10 9 8 7 6 5 4 3 2 1

Frontispiece: Jean-François Millet, *The Gleaners* (1857).
Photo © Musée d'Orsay, Dist. RMN-Grand Palais / Patrice Schmidt.

ALSO BY ILANA PARDES

Countertraditions in the Bible:
A Feminist Approach

The Biography of Ancient Israel:
National Narratives in the Bible

New Perspectives on Freud's Moses and Monotheism
(editor, with Ruth Ginsburg)

Melville's Bibles

Agnon's Moonstruck Lovers:
The Song of Songs in Israeli Culture

The Book of Job: Aesthetics, Ethics, Hermeneutics
(editor, with Leora Batnitzky)

The Song of Songs: A Biography

Psalms In/On Jerusalem (editor,
with Ophir Münz-Manor)

For Keren and Eyal with love

CONTENTS

RUTH

Preliminary Gleanings

THE BOOK OF RUTH offers the most elaborate tale of a woman to be found in the Bible, but even this relatively detailed account is astonishingly spare. The book of Ruth is not really a book. It is only four chapters long—more of a short story, or a very short story, than a book. To write a biography of Ruth thus means to become a gleaner, to gather bits and pieces from sparse scenes that are replete with lacunae. And yet, despite its ellipses, Ruth's cryptic tale is remarkable for its capacity to provide, with but few vignettes, a vibrant portrait of one of the most intriguing characters in the Bible.

The opening note of the book of Ruth is devoted to a packed expository account of the migration of Elimelech's family from the land of Judah to Moab. Much like Abraham and Jacob, who go down to Egypt in times of famine, Elimelech migrates to a foreign land in quest of sustenance. He is accompanied by his wife, Naomi, and their two sons, Mahlon and Chilion. It is a dire migratory tale. Elimelech dies shortly after their move, and ten years later the two sons die as well. Ruth is first mentioned in this prelude as Mahlon's Moabite wife, alongside Orpah, Chilion's Moabite wife. We receive no information about her lineage or background. The Midrash fills in this lacuna and endows Ruth with royal attributes, turning her into a princess, one of the daughters of Eglon, king of Moab. But in the biblical text itself, Ruth's Moabite past seems to have no relevance. Even more striking, Ruth's marriage to Mahlon and their childless years together receive no attention. Ruth may have felt as desperate as the barren Rachel does when crying to Jacob, "Give me children, or else I die."[1] But the narrative does not dwell on Ruth's marital life, nor does it reveal anything about her response to the death of her husband. Instead we shift from the prelude to another story of migration—where the drama begins—this time in the opposite direction, from Moab to Bethlehem.

Ruth emerges onstage only on the road between Moab and Bethlehem, after leaving her home and homeland to head to the land of Judah, a land she had not known hitherto. Her migration is as radical as that of Abraham's inaugural move to Canaan but different in character. No God calls out of nowhere and demands that she go forth. Going forth is her own initiative, and her primary objective is not to obey God but rather to stand by Naomi. With remarkable flair, Ruth endorses *hesed*, kindness, as her guideline, willing to take all the risks involved in following her impoverished, melancholy mother-in-law to a foreign land.[2]

Ruth's tale of migration is an unusual one. Elsewhere in the Bible, in the great stories of migration in Genesis and Exodus, male characters are the ones to prevail; here, a woman is set center stage, and the specificities of the life of a female migrant are spelled out with distinct verve. We follow Ruth through the various stages of her migratory life, from the moment she leaves Moab as a childless widow, determined to join Naomi, through the circuitous process of acculturation in Bethlehem, beginning with her struggle to survive as a gleaner in the barley fields and ending with her marriage to a "local," Boaz, and her giving birth to Obed.

What makes Ruth's migratory tale all the more exceptional is that she is a Moabite. It is the story of a Moabite woman who, on moving to Bethlehem, becomes not only a member of the people of Israel but also the foremother of King David. This dramatic shift in Ruth's position is one of the greatest enigmas of her life: How could a foreign woman become a founding figure of the Davidic dynasty? What is her charm? What makes her indispensable?

Ruth's tale is set "in the days when the judges ruled" (Ruth 1:1).[3] The "judges," the *shoftim*, are tribal chieftains who ruled in the pre-monarchic period, presumably from the thirteenth century to the eleventh century BCE. Despite this historical note in the first verse, we might well wonder if Ruth is a historical figure or a figment of the imagination. There are no archaeological findings or extrabiblical texts that corroborate her existence. This lack of evidence, however, does not prove that Ruth never set foot in the fields of Bethlehem. It is hard to imagine any scribe daring to position a Moabite woman at the base of the Davidic dynasty if there were not some basis in historical reality. But whether or not Ruth was a genuine historical figure, the book of Ruth treats her as such. The God of Israel reveals himself in history and carries out his plans through and against real people. A historical impulse informs the Bible, though this impulse surely differs from modern notions of historiography.

History in the Bible goes hand in hand with literature. In fact, narrative is the prevalent mode for recording past events in the biblical text. Features that today would be perceived as the domain of literature—elaborate studies of human relationships, dialogues no one could have heard, inner thoughts, depictions of emotional responses—are regarded in the biblical context as vital to the understanding of historical realities.[4] Commenting on biblical scholars who insist on distinguishing between fact and fiction in Moses's life, Martin Buber reflects on the futility of such endeavors. Instead of trying to find clear boundaries between history and literature, Buber calls for a consideration of the power of the experience of an actual foundational event or an actual encounter with a prominent historical figure to generate literature. Poetry and sagas may seem to be far from historical truth, but in fact, in their own distinct way they preserve the memories of the initial, intense emotional response to the unexpected qualities of historical events and personae.[5] We are familiar with similar phenomena in later contexts as well. Abraham Lincoln, Theodor Herzl, and Mahatma Gandhi are historical figures, and yet they hold a position as legendary leaders in our cultural memory. Although Ruth is not a leader or a judge (if we think in terms of her historical setting), perhaps those who met her felt that her exceptional life mattered, that her tale needed to be passed on.[6]

The association of Ruth with the time of the judges is rather odd since her tale seems to be the antithesis of the representation of this period in the book of Judges. The well-known and recurrent verse of Judges is "Every man did what was right in his own eyes." It is an age in which lawlessness and strife prevail. Ad hoc tribal chieftains, the shoftim, attempt to rescue the weak confederation of Hebrew tribes from their enemies, but shortly after each battle, even the most successful ones, chaos returns. With its unique ambience, the book of Ruth offers an alternative human possibility, or, perhaps, a glimpse of a different chapter within this period. We enter Bethlehem in the days of harvest, with no shadow of an enemy on the horizon. People greet one another with respect in the fields, and legal matters are settled peacefully at the town's gate.

There are no villains in the book of Ruth. In fact, one of the tale's stunning literary feats is its convincing portrayal of good people. It is a rare world in which hesed emerges as a cherished principle of human relations. Ruth is the primary agent of hesed, and she is hailed for it time and again. But other characters are also construed as kind and compassionate. Even Orpah, who, unlike Ruth, decides to head back to Moab instead of following her mother-in-law to Bethlehem, is not wicked. Naomi thanks Orpah for her hesed and care while urging her to return to her mother's house. She is a good person, just less good than Ruth. God too has a pivotal role in advancing hesed, but he remains behind the scenes. He is not really a character and his voice is not heard. It is primarily human agency and human goodness that shape the drama in the book of Ruth.

In a talk on goodness, delivered in 2012, the novelist Toni Morrison points out that "contemporary literature is not interested in goodness on a large or even limited scale. When it appears, it is with a note of apology in its hand and has trouble speaking its name."[7] Critical of this tendency, she harks back to nineteenth-century writers who did not hesitate to explore the far from bland lives of good people. Biblical narrative, strangely enough, is not that different from modern literature in its suspicion of goodness. More often than not, the biographies of prominent biblical figures are replete with scenes of jealousy, cheating, and violence. Jacob tricks his brother, Esau, and his father, Isaac, in order to become the chosen heir; Leah and Rachel engage in fierce struggles over Jacob's love; Joseph's brothers fling him into the pit; David sends Uriah to his death in order to conceal his affair with Bathsheba. Ruth's tale, with its substantive attention to goodness, is a rare exception. Ruth, in a sense, is a precursor of Herman Melville's Billy Budd and even more so of George Eliot's Dorothea Brooke, the protagonist of *Middlemarch*, whose unconditional devotion to her husband, Casaubon, is one of the most intriguing aspects of the novel. Good characters are not flawless nor are their lives necessarily less miserable or devoid of tensions, but they have a unique light, an unimaginable generosity, that compels all who surround them, even those who try to deny their fascination.

When this tale of hesed was composed remains a mystery. That the events took place in the days of the judges does not mean that it was written in this period. The concluding genealogy of the book of Ruth, with its reference to King David at the end of the line, indicates a much later date of composition. Many modern scholars have regarded the book of Ruth as a polemical text composed in the fifth century BCE as an argument against the exclusionary policy on foreign wives then being propagated by Ezra and Nehemiah. These scholars rely on linguistic phenomena—the appearance of certain words that belong to the later strata of biblical Hebrew—as well as on content: the favorable representation of a foreign woman. And yet this method of dating has its complications. The linguistic evidence attests to the period of the final editing, but earlier versions of Ruth's tale may have circulated in the pre-monarchic era, or during the reign of King David.[8] What is more, the matching of what is construed as the ideology of the text with a given historical setting cannot be decisive. Condemnations of intermarriage and foreign women are delivered in a whole array of biblical texts across multiple historical contexts. The text could have been composed in the time of Ezra and Nehemiah, but it need not have been. Any attempt to yoke the book of Ruth to clearcut political purposes is as erroneous as regarding the book of Samuel as either pro-Davidic or anti-Davidic. Rather than endorsing a given agenda, the book of Ruth provides an insightful account of the life of a migrant woman. And like any profound meditation on humanity, it refrains from idealization. While offering a remarkably positive perspective on a foreign woman, Ruth's tale is not innocent of moments of ambivalence. Ruth is embraced by the people of Bethlehem, but in more subtle ways the shadow of her Moabite origin lurks in the background. Acculturation has its limits.

Much as the dating of the book of Ruth is unknown so is the identity of its author or authors. A Talmudic tradition attributes the authorship of the book to the prophet Samuel. In the realm of modern scholarship, we find a variety of opinions. Alongside those who assume that the writer was a supporter of intermarriage in the days of Ezra and Nehemiah are others who trace in Ruth's tale the imprint of a "wise woman" (analogous to the wise woman of 2 Samuel 14:2).[9] Still others have suggested that the book was transmitted orally by female storytellers before it was set in writing. Even if women were not among the biblical scribes, their oral tales could potentially have seeped into the canon deliberately or unintentionally.[10] Claims that the book of Ruth is the product of feminine imagination are attuned to the considerable space allotted to women's perspectives in this tale, but however compelling they remain speculative. The power of great writers is often revealed in their capacity to cross boundaries and dive into realms that lie beyond their immediate experiences. This is true of gender boundaries as well: Gustave Flaubert does not hesitate to flesh out the details of Madame Bovary's world and Virginia Woolf whimsically imagines Orlando's life both as a man and as a woman.

The task of a biographer is usually to choose out of a plethora of documents the most pertinent ones, to construct a new narrative from known sources as well as previously unknown archival materials. Writing a biography of Ruth is an atypical endeavor. Our only primary source is the book of Ruth, and even this lone source cannot be pinned down as far as its dating and authorship. What we do have, however, is an intricate network of links between Ruth and other biblical figures that thickens her portrait. No biblical character is an island. Every biblical figure is inextricably connected to other characters, not only through familial ties but also by means of recurrent patterns. Ruth's life is primarily intertwined with that of Naomi, her mother-in-law, but her story also embodies traces of the lives of women from the distant past. In the concluding chapter of the book, the elders at the town gate bless Ruth as one who is destined to follow in the footsteps of the matriarchs Rachel and Leah, as well as Tamar. This is not only a future-oriented blessing. In the various scenes that precede the ceremony at the gate, Ruth's actions are already cast, if implicitly, in relation to those of the three founding female figures of Genesis. Other links are more hidden. One such link is between Ruth and her notorious Moabite foremother, Lot's daughter, who seduced her own father (with the help of her sister) after the destruction of Sodom. Through another implicit allusion, Ruth's migration is made analogous to that of Abraham. And more diffusely, we find certain affinities between Ruth and the migrant Joseph.

I begin this biography with my own detailed reading, or rather retelling, of the book of Ruth. My reading is attuned to the dramatic qualities of Ruth's tale—to the exquisite dialogues, the chief instrument for revealing the relations of the personages. It follows the reported details but devotes as much attention, if not more, to what is not said, to the many lacunae of the text. While oscillating between what is revealed and what remains unspoken in the background, I probe a network of interconnections between Ruth's tale and the tales of other biblical characters. I also consider references to the Bible's legal corpus, an intricate nexus of diverse laws, from the law of gleaning to the levirate law to the law of redemption. These laws are neither dry nor technical. Embedded in the narrative, they are among the features that add much color to Ruth's life.

Throughout my reading, I devote special attention to the nuanced charting of Ruth's life as a migrant woman. In highlighting the migratory dimension of the book, I explore the theme that seems to me the most compelling for our own twenty-first-century concerns. I regard this ancient tale as an incredibly rich turf for the exploration of migratory experiences that remain only too relevant today: the acute sense of uprootedness, the struggle to find sustenance in a foreign land, the resilience and audacity that are required in order to survive, the yearnings for home, and the quest for a new beginning. My aim, however, is not to erase historical differences. I am attuned to the specific conditions of migrants, and women migrants in particular, in the biblical context. My use of the term *migrant* rather than *immigrant* to define the biblical Ruth is indicative. *Migration* is a broader term that is not associated solely with modern nation-states and as such is more appropriate in treating biblical characters.

The bulk of this biography, however, revolves around Ruth's readers. Numerous readers from diverse cultural and religious backgrounds and across many centuries have been charmed by Ruth and determined to reinterpret her tale. We'll explore some of Ruth's most captivating afterlives: she appears as a convert in the Midrash, as the Shekhinah in exile in the Zohar, as a pastoral gleaner in French art, as a pioneer in early Zionism, and as a paradigmatic stranger and outcast in renditions of the twentieth and twenty-first centuries. Reflecting on a text's "life" and "afterlife," the philosopher Walter Benjamin claims that an afterlife "could not be called that if it were not a transformation and a renewal of something living—the original undergoes a change."[11] Through its transformation—or rather its incessant transformations—a text is brought back to life, acquiring new meanings, some of which would have been unimaginable to earlier generations. Benjamin addresses the question of afterlives in the context of translation, the relationship between an original work and its translations. But his observations are equally pertinent to the afterlives of characters. In each episode of Ruth's reception history, she undergoes a cultural translation as she is made relevant within a new milieu. In the wake of Benjamin, we may say that Ruth's varied afterlives do not only reveal much about their own times; they also shine light upon the biblical text, transforming, renewing, and extending the enigmas of the ancient gleaner's primary life.

The question of migration will continue to be pivotal as we wander among Ruth's afterlives. In every exegetical scene along the way, we'll consider the shifting perspectives on Ruth's foreignness. We'll explore the attempts of the rabbis to domesticate Ruth's foreign origin by turning her into an exemplary convert, and the Zohar's insistence that Ruth's Moabite background is vital to her redemptive powers as an embodiment of the Shekhinah. In moving to early-modern and modern French art, we'll look at pastoral paintings of the ancient gleaner, in which Ruth's foreign origin is relegated to the margins or obfuscated altogether. We'll follow the European pastoral gleaner as she crosses over to Zionist fields in the early twentieth century and becomes a pioneer. The final chapters, devoted to the reception of Ruth's tale in the Israeli and American contexts, review modernist and contemporary readings in literature, photography, and film in which Ruth's literal and figurative dislocations are brought into relief and are seen as part of her aesthetic and ethical legacy.

The concluding chapters lead us to readings that are closer to my own in their attention to the migratory dimension of the tale. While giving them more space, my goal is not to refute the validity of previous trends. Each afterlife has its own lure if we consider the changing conditions or crises that made it urgent. Reflecting on the long exegetical history of Ruth's tale will allow us to gain a historical perspective and deepen our understanding of current interpretive choices. Above all, plunging into the world of Ruth's afterlives will allow us to savor the wondrous freedom of interpretative endeavors: the unending ways in which Ruth the Moabite may live anew.

1

The Moabite

THE DRAMA BEGINS on the road between Moab and Bethlehem with a scene of three women on the move: Naomi, Ruth,
and Orpah. We receive no details regarding the appearance or
attire of these women. Impoverished as they were and embarking on a journey to Bethlehem in quest of sustenance, they were
probably dressed in rags. They had none of the familiar biblical
tokens of wealth: no saddled donkeys, no servants. We do not
know how long they walked on the road or whether they talked
with other sojourners. To those who watched them pass they
must have seemed an exceptional sight. Women did not travel
on their own in biblical times unless they were in dire circumstances. The road was a male zone. Where exactly were the
women when they began to converse? We are not told. Instead
of providing us with elementary expository details, the narrative zooms in on a moment of crisis. We can imagine the three
wayfarers halting for a moment as Naomi begins to speak. Bur-

dened by her sorrows, Naomi now seems to have second thoughts about her daughters-in-law coming to Bethlehem with her, for she urges them to return to Moab:

> "Go back, each of you to her mother's house. May the Lord do kindness with you as you have done with the dead and with me. May the Lord grant that you find a settled place, each of you in the house of her husband." And she kissed them, and they raised their voice and wept. And they said to her, "But with you we will go back to your people." And Naomi said, "Go back, my daughters, why should you go with me? Do I still have sons in my womb who could be husbands to you? Go back, my daughters, go, for I am too old to have a husband. Even had I thought 'I have hope. This very night I shall have a husband and bear sons,' would you wait for them till they grew up? For them would you be deprived of husbands? No, my daughters, for it is far more bitter for me than for you because the Lord's hand has come out against me." (1:8–13)

Clinging to an elderly widow whose womb is "empty," Naomi painfully admits, makes no sense. The sons whom she bore have died, and she is too old to begin anew. For a brief moment, she wildly imagines finding a new husband "this very night" and bearing new sons. But then she dismisses her own fantasy, asking her daughters-in-law whether they would absurdly wait for her imaginary future sons to grow up. Regretting her initial desire to be accompanied by them, she now thanks her daughters-in-law for their kindness, their hesed, and pleads with them to go back to the homes of their Moabite mothers. Depleted as she is, in body and soul, she has nothing to offer. Her piercing rhetorical questions are meant to shatter any illusion that this journey could provide a better future. Migrating to an unknown land would only augment their misery, she insists, limiting their chances of settling down and building new families.

The emotional intensity of this scene increases as Ruth and

Orpah raise their voices and weep (1:14). They cry, we may assume, over the losses and hardships they all share in common, but they also cry at the thought of separating, severing the remainders of a bereaved family. Orpah ends up following Naomi's advice and returns to Moab. Her name, *orpa* (calling to mind the word *oref*, "nape"), seems to commemorate her decision to turn back. But Orpah is by no means heartless. She chooses the commonsensical path in a world run by men, in which a widow is among the most helpless and underprivileged, synonymous with the stranger and the orphan.[1] However painful being a widow today may be, it does not necessarily entail a loss of income or status. Within the biblical context, however, a widow is by definition lowly, economically and socially. Being both a widow and a stranger is undoubtedly even worse.

Unlike Orpah, Ruth is not swayed by the fear of the double misfortune that may await her on migrating to the land of Judah. She opts for the road less traveled by and remains with her destitute mother-in-law. Her hesed, we discover, exceeds familiar definitions of compassion and goodness. The meaning of the name "Ruth"—*rut*, as it is pronounced in Hebrew—is uncertain. But it may be associated with the term *re'ut*, "friend," or more specifically, "female companion," thus calling attention to Ruth's unique traits.[2]

THE OATH ON THE ROAD: BETWEEN MOAB AND BETHLEHEM

It is at this climactic moment on the road, as the two sisters-in-law move in opposite directions, that Ruth emerges as a distinct character, speaking for the first time on her own. She delivers the most resonant lines of the tale with great passion and stubborn audacity:

> Do not entreat me to forsake you, to turn back from you. For wherever you go, I will go. And wherever you lodge, I will lodge. Your people is my people, and your god is my god.

Wherever you die, I will die, and there will I be buried. So
may the Lord do to me or even more, for only death will part
you and me. (1:16–17)

Ruth's moving oath of love and loyalty is so well known, so oft
cited that its beauty and power might go unnoticed. Earlier,
Ruth's words merged with those of Orpah (1:10), but now that
her sister-in-law has left, Ruth speaks differently—shifting from
prose to poetry, using parallel clauses (parallelism is the predominant feature of biblical poetry). When biblical narrative
introduces brief poetic insets into the prose it often marks a
heightened moment, a dramatic scene that calls for special attention.[3] Ruth's oath is one such moment. The majestic opening
parallelism, with its rhythmic force and emphatic repetition—
"For wherever you go I will go"—sets the tone for the rest.
Ruth's insistence on going with Naomi is nothing short of total.
It means lodging wherever Naomi lodges, even if her mother-
in-law finds no real abode in Bethlehem; it means going so far
as to adopt her mother-in-law's people and God as her own.
Only death will part them, but in a sense not even death—for
Ruth is determined to be buried wherever her mother-in-law is
buried.

Ruth's exceptional oath, however, would not have granted
her entry into Bethlehem had it not included a commitment
to Naomi's God and people. In modern scenes of migration,
potential immigrants are meticulously inspected by the authorities of their host country to verify that they meet required criteria. Marrying a citizen is often considered a viable criterion. In
the biblical text, the prospect of acceptance through marriage
is more ambiguous. Intermarriage is usually condemned, which
is why there are no official guidelines. Nonetheless, in practice
intermarriage is often regarded as permissible—from Moses's
marriage to the Midianite Zipporah to David's entourage of
foreign wives. The implicit precept seems to be that foreign

wives are accepted as long as they do not violate the monotheistic underpinnings of life and are willing to efface their
cultural past.

The daughters of Moab have a dubious reputation in this
regard. When the wandering Israelites finally reached the plains
of Moab on the threshold of the Promised Land, they went
"whoring" with the daughters of Moab, who seduced them into
taking part in the sacrificial meals offered to the Canaanite god,
Baal Peor (Numbers 25:1). Influenced by the daughters of Moab,
the Israelites "clung" (*vayitsamed*) to the idol as they followed
the enticing women they had discovered beyond the wilderness. Ruth's conduct is the very antithesis of that of her Moabite precursors in Numbers. On crossing the border between
Moab and the land of Judah, she embraces Naomi's God and
people, passing the admission test to the land of Judah.[4]

Ruth is a model daughter-in-law and a model migrant, but
her phenomenal declaration of loyalty is not lauded by Naomi.
Instead of falling in Ruth's arms and expressing her gratitude,
Naomi does not utter a word. Characters in the Bible, as Robert Alter points out, are "often unpredictable, in some ways im-
penetrable, constantly emerging from and slipping back into a
penumbra of ambiguity."[5] One of the wonders of biblical narrative, in fact, lies in its invitation—or rather, its demand—that
we explore silences and consider divergent possibilities of mo-
tive and emotional response. Although the biblical narrator is
omniscient, we as readers are not. We must learn about characters the same way we learn about the people in our daily lives—
through ongoing observation and conjecture. We may surmise
that Naomi's choice to cease talking with Ruth on the road discloses her ambivalence. Despite her genuine care for her daughter-
in-law, she may be reluctant to have her by her side. Is Naomi
troubled, now that they are approaching Bethlehem, by Ruth's
Moabite origin? Is she worried about the reaction of the people
of Bethlehem to her foreign daughter-in-law?[6] Perhaps. But there

is another interpretive route. We might equally assume that her silence is a mark of her deep melancholy. Miserable as Naomi is, she may be feeling unworthy of her daughter-in-law's compassion or else incapable of delighting in the remarkable gift of hesed offered to her. These diverse readings are not mutually exclusive: Naomi may be both ambivalent and melancholy, both loving and withdrawn. Whatever the reasons for her silence may be, the two women continue to walk together to Bethlehem, and Naomi no longer tries to dissuade Ruth.

Strictly speaking, only Ruth is a migrant who enters an unknown town, but in many ways Naomi too is a migrant, or even a double migrant. Her first migration was to Moab—and now, on returning to Bethlehem after ten years away and the disasters that befell her, she feels acutely uprooted yet again. Ruth and Naomi share the stage in intricate ways—each contributing different aspects to this tale of migration. Whereas Ruth is more poignantly the foreigner, the Moabite, who joins a people she has not known heretofore, Naomi expresses more extensively the inner tumult of self-estrangement. The penultimate verse of the opening chapter underscores their inseparability: "And Naomi came back, and her daughter-in-law with her who was coming back from the plains of Moab" (1:22). As surprising as it might at first seem, Ruth, much like Naomi, is considered to be "returning" to her homeland, though she has never set foot in the land of Judah before. Much as they share a homecoming, they also share their respective migrations.[7]

The "whole town" is "astir" as the two women arrive in Bethlehem. In this exceptional text, in which women's agency is foregrounded, Bethlehem too is perceived—at first sight, at least—as a feminine world. It is the women of Bethlehem who approach them. Rushing toward Naomi, they ask, "Is this Naomi?" They probably find it difficult to recognize her after all these years. But Naomi regards their question in a different register, as relevant to her deep sense of estrangement: "Do not call me Naomi. Call me Mara, for Shaddai [the Almighty] has dealt great bitterness to me. I went out full, and empty did the Lord bring me back. Why should you call me Naomi when the Lord has borne witness against me and Shaddai has done me harm?" (1:20–21). She conveys her inner alienation by dissociating herself from her name, the quintessential marker of identity. The name "Naomi" (akin to "pleasant") no longer suits her, she laments: a more appropriate name would be "Mara"— the bitter one. Not unlike Job, Naomi protests against a God who has tortured her mercilessly for no apparent reason.[8] Once again there is a shift from prose to poetry, underscoring the emotional intensity of the moment. In a forceful parallelism, Naomi juxtaposes her emptiness to the fullness with which she was blessed on leaving for Moab: "I went out full, and empty did the Lord bring me back." If earlier, on the road, she spoke of God's hand leveled against her (1:13), now that she has returned without her husband and sons to an empty home, she spells out her complaint toward the heavens in bold strokes. She portrays herself as a defendant in an unjust legal court: the punishment has already been executed, and yet the charges and the evidence remain disturbingly unknown.

No one responds to Naomi's defiant cry, neither the women of Bethlehem nor Ruth. Perhaps they realize that no words can alleviate Naomi's anguish, much as Job's companions (who had come to console him) sat with him on the ground for seven days and seven nights, "and none spoke a word to him, for they saw that the pain was very great" (Job 2:13). Ruth's silence, however, may also be seen as a token of her deep identification with Naomi. Naomi's cry must have captured something of Ruth's own pain as a childless widow entering the streets of a strange town. Ruth's thoughts remain unexpressed, but she may be feeling all the more displaced as she realizes that the women of Bethlehem, much like Naomi, seem to utterly ignore her presence. In its distinct cryptic mode, the book of Ruth does not allow us to forget the unbearable rifts at the heart of migratory lives, even as it places greater emphasis on the craving to construct a new home and seek a new beginning.

The first chapter ends with a comment: "And they had come to Bethlehem at the beginning of the barley harvest" (1:22). This concluding note seems to offer a dim sign or hint of a potential future transition from a scene of mourning, hunger, and estrangement to a world of bread and plentitude. If in the opening of the tale there was a discrepancy between the significance of "Bethlehem"—a name that means "house of bread"—and the famine that had struck the land, now the town of Bethlehem seems likely to be restored to its former glory. The rumor Naomi heard while she was still in Moab that "the Lord had singled out His people to give them bread" (1:6) was not groundless.

There is a glimmer of hope in this final line but no theodicy. The narrator makes no attempt to justify God's ways or explicate the reasons for the innocent suffering we have witnessed. The statement is purely descriptive, marking the inevitable ebb and flow of human life. Much as God can inflict famine so too he can provide bread. At this point of the tale it is unclear whether God's renewed benevolence toward Bethlehem will mitigate the sorrows of Ruth and Naomi. When Abraham descended to Egypt in times of famine he returned from his sojourns with much property. Naomi, by contrast, has returned empty-handed, with no material goods whatsoever. Nor is there any indication that she is even able to return to her former house. Where Naomi and Ruth lodge in Bethlehem remains unknown.

And yet the potentialities of a different future hover in the air. Could Naomi's name, like that of Bethlehem, suit her once again? Does the fertility of the land intimate that human fertility may be restored? Will this estranged town become more of a home for both Ruth and Naomi?

GLEANING IN ALIEN FIELDS: THE FIRST STEPS

Shortly after their arrival in Bethlehem, Ruth heads to the barley fields. Her migrant's tale—like that of most migrants, then and now—revolves around a search for work and sustenance in the new land. Ruth's boldness on the road is now apparent in Bethlehem. Determined to solve their most immediate problem—hunger—she turns to her mother-in-law and says, "Let me go, pray, to the field, and glean from among the ears of grain after I find favor in his eyes" (2:2). Ruth does not yet know in whose field she will glean, but she realizes from the outset that it is essential to "find favor" in the eyes of the landowner. Foreigners are vulnerable and must calculate their steps with caution as they try to find work. Naomi does not join Ruth, because she is either paralyzed by grief or too old for the task.

"The foreigner," writes Julia Kristeva, "is the one who works. . . . You will recognize the foreigner in that he *still* considers work as a value. A vital necessity, to be sure, his sole means of survival, on which he does not necessarily place a halo of glory but simply claims as a primary right, the zero degree of dignity."[9] Given that finding a job is far more urgent for foreigners, they tend to be highly ambitious, ready to take any job, and even to invent new ones. Many migrant tales revolve around lowly beginnings, the struggle to find a means of survival, the difficulties of acquiring a new language and coping with inevitable humiliations. Then, at least in the happy versions, comes a dramatic transition: from working in stony fields and stifling sweatshops to becoming rich and affluent, spearheading financial, scientific, or cultural changes no one has dreamed of before.

The rags-to-riches migrant tale of the successful entrepreneur is, however, primarily a male model, and was all the more so in the ancient world. When Joseph is brought down to Egypt as a slave, he manages against all odds to make his way to the top. First, Joseph "finds favor" in Potiphar's eyes and is placed in charge of his master's house (Genesis 39:4). Later he climbs the social ladder and acquires an influential position in Pharaoh's court. Deeply impressed by Joseph's unique wisdom, Pharaoh designates him as his top adviser and administrator and endows him with the power to rule in his name "over all the land of Egypt" (Genesis 41:42–43). Joseph is precisely the kind of hardworking migrant with vision who can engineer an economic revolution in Egypt that no one else could have imagined.

Ruth's tale is a woman's migrant tale, and as such its trajectory is considerably different. Women as a rule are not an integral part of the workplace in the biblical world. Maidens appear occasionally as reapers or shepherds, but by and large women are relegated to the domestic sphere. Gleaning is a category of its own, the kind of work that is available to destitute people who have no one to support them. The right to glean is granted by the biblical welfare system and is intended to supply the most impoverished—the stranger (or sojourner), the orphan, and the widow—with a minimal source of sustenance.[10] Far from being a dry decree, the law of gleaning in Deuteronomy is based on an ethical call to acknowledge suffering through identification: "And you shall remember that you were a slave in Egypt, and the Lord your God ransomed you from there. Therefore do I charge you to do this thing. When you reap your harvest in your field and forget a sheaf in the field, you shall not go back to take it. For the sojourner and for the orphan and for the widow it shall be, so that the Lord your God may bless you in all the work of your hands" (Deuteronomy 24:18–19).[11] Knowing only too well what being wretched means, the people of Israel are required to ensure the well-being of the outcasts and strangers in their midst. Interestingly enough, the leftover sheaves in the fields are not simply given to the poor as an act of charity: they must toil for such social benefits. The framing of the law makes the requirement less of an expense for the owners, but it also has the poor in mind. Gleaners are given the opportunity to take an active role in securing their own livelihood. Unlike reapers, they do not get paid for their work, but gleaning provides them (or is meant to provide them) with enough food to sustain themselves.

Ruth has the right to glean both as a widow and as a stranger, but she does not take this right for granted. Her conduct in the field is exemplary. Ruth asks for permission before she begins to glean and then limits herself to gathering only leftover ears of grain that have fallen from the sheaves, which is why she remains "behind the reapers" (2:3). To top it all, Ruth's diligence is exceptional, "standing" as she does in the fields from the morning on, presumably without a moment of rest (2:7). Within the limits of what women migrants could achieve in the biblical world, Ruth manages to do precisely what Joseph does in Potiphar's house and later in Pharaoh's palace: find favor, be singled out in a way that allows her, gradually, to gain unexpected privileges.

A touch of romance is introduced into this scene when the field owner, Boaz,[12] appears and asks the overseer, "Whose is this young woman [na'arah]?" (2:5). We now learn that although Ruth is a widow, she looks young, appearing to Boaz as a na-'arah, a young, nubile woman. The use of "whose" discloses his assumption that she must be under the authority of her father's house. After Boaz hears the overseer's favorable account of the young Moabite gleaner, his interest in Ruth is aroused further, and he ventures to address her directly: "And Boaz said to Ruth, 'Have you not heard, my daughter—do not go to glean in another field, and also do not pass on from here, and so shall you cling to my young women. Your eyes be on the field in which they reap and go after them. . . . Should you be thirsty, you shall go to the pitchers and drink from what the lads draw from the well'" (2:8–9).

Boaz endows Ruth with a privileged position among the

gleaners. Ruth is invited to join the young women who reap in his field and is granted permission to ask the lads to draw water from the well should she be thirsty.[13] In responding to Boaz's generosity, Ruth must remain humble: "And she fell on her face and bowed to the ground and said to him, 'Why should I find favor in your eyes to recognize me [*lehakireni*] when I am a foreigner [*nokhriya*]?'" (2:10). Ruth's use of the term *nokhriya* (foreigner) is an interesting choice. The Bible distinguishes between *ger* and *nokhri*. The ger is a precursor of today's "resident alien," a stranger who is considered a member of the community, though not a full member. As such, the ger is required to abide by some of the principal Israelite laws and has certain rights, among them the right to glean and the right to rest on the Sabbath. The nokhri, by contrast, is a foreigner who is not part of the Israelite community, but the term may also designate a figurative, internal sense of alienation.[14] In legal terms, Ruth is closer to the position of the ger, but in choosing to define herself as a nokhriya, she underscores her sense of acute estrangement on making her first steps in an unknown land. Her self-deprecation, however, may also be seen as an attempt to be cautious in dealing with those in power. When the fugitive David encounters Saul in one of the caves of Ein-gedi, he declares, "After whom has the king of Israel come forth, after whom are you chasing? After a dead dog, after a single flea?" (1 Samuel 24:15). Ruth is not as wily as her descendant, but she realizes what migrants and fugitives must realize if they want to survive: that self-deprecation is a vital strategy.

While belittling herself, Ruth compliments Boaz. Her rhetorical ingenuity is evident in her juggling of two antithetical words, *recognize* and *foreigner*, that share the same root: *n kh r*. Instead of ignoring her, playing the stranger to the stranger (*nokhriya*), he ventures to recognize her (*lehakireni*). A more standard reply to Boaz's generosity would have been a humble note of gratitude. But Ruth complicates her praise as she lays

THE MOABITE

bare the grim truth: strangers usually remain invisible. Why then has Boaz chosen to "recognize" her, to treat her as visible? This is not a complaint, of course, but a way of highlighting Boaz's unusual choice while urging him to reflect on it. And— yes—there is something flirtatious in Ruth's question: she lures Boaz into thinking of her and continuing the conversation.

There is a spark between the two. Boaz's response has its own flair. Spelling out his reasons for "recognizing" her, he depicts Ruth's conduct as nothing less than Abrahamic in stature:

> And Boaz answered and said, "It was indeed told me, all that you did for your mother-in-law after your husband's death, and that you left your mother and your father and the land of your birth to come to a people that you did not know in time past. May the LORD requite your actions and may your reward be complete from the LORD God of Israel under Whose wings you have come to shelter." (2:11–12)

Boaz's words call to mind the inaugural divine message to Abraham in Genesis: "Go forth [*lekh lekha*] from your land and your birthplace and your father's house to the land I will show you. And I will make you a great nation and I will bless you and make your name great, and you shall be a blessing" (12:1–3). The analogy Boaz draws between Ruth and Abraham adds grandeur to the Moabite's migration to the land of Judah, as it underscores the audacity and the sacrifice entailed in severing one's closest ties and moving to a strange new place. Ruth, Boaz insists, is no lowly foreigner but rather an admirable woman whose capacity for rupture—to leave home and homeland—is as monumental as that of the founding patriarch of the Israelites. That she left Moab for the sake of her mother-in-law makes her all the more worthy of being rewarded by God.

Ruth cannot but be moved by Boaz's wholehearted acknowledgment of her deeds: "And she said, 'May I find favor in the eyes of my lord, for you have comforted me and have spoken to the heart of your servant when I could scarcely be like one of your slavegirls'" (2:13). Ruth admits that Boaz has "comforted" her (*nihamtani*), implying that his kind words have alleviated some of the agonies she has experienced as a migrant widow. She goes so far as to intimate that he has touched her heart but remains careful, claiming that she does not even deserve to be one of his slaves.

A lovely idyllic moment follows: "And Boaz said to her at mealtime, 'Come here and eat of the bread and dip your crust in vinegar.' And she sat alongside the reapers, and he bundled together roasted grain for her, and she ate and was sated and left some over" (2:14). It seems like a hungry migrant's wishful dream. Bread comes bountifully, so much that Ruth "left some over." And what makes this bread all the more delightful is the addition of vinegar, the biblical equivalent of a savory dip. The hunger that haunts the opening episode now seems to have vanished. Better still, Boaz provides Ruth not only with much-needed food but also with much-needed human warmth. Ruth is welcomed into the reapers' circle, though she modestly sits near the reapers rather than among them. And then, in an endearing gesture, Boaz prepares a bundle of roasted grain just for her. Immediately following this meal, Boaz orders his workmen to allow Ruth to gather leftovers not only behind the reapers but also "among the sheaves" (2:15). What is more, he urges them to leave some sheaves for Ruth on purpose and refrain from reproaching her (2:16). Boaz goes beyond the letter of the law, but his admirable generosity has its limits. He does not mention the fact that he is a kinsman of Elimelech and as such might have an even greater responsibility toward the new gleaner in his field.

When Ruth returns to town, she gives her mother-in-law "what she had left over after being sated" (2:18). Ruth's earlier resolve to preserve some of the bounty allows her to share the goods with Naomi. The oath on the road acquires a new form in Bethlehem. My sheaves of barley, she indicates in her deeds, are yours, much as my bit of luck is yours. Ruth's continual devotion to Naomi seems to seep into her mother-in-law's heart. "Where did you glean today and where did you work?" asks Naomi, going on to declare, "May he who recognized you be blessed!" (2:19). Without being in the fields, Naomi, like Ruth, defines the benefactor as one who "recognizes" (*makirekh*) those who are down and out. And on hearing that the field owner is none other than Boaz, Naomi seems to be all the more encouraged. If on her entry to Bethlehem, the Job-like, melancholy Naomi comes close to cursing God, at this point she blesses Boaz and expresses gratitude for divine hesed: "Blessed is he to the Lord, Who has not forsaken His kindness with the living and with the dead!" (2:20). God is no longer a torturer but rather a merciful benefactor whose hesed is reflected in human hesed.

Naomi's sudden joy is not limited to the grain that now begins to fill her emptiness. In a laconic remark, she informs Ruth that her chance encounter with Boaz is of special significance because he is their relative, a "redeeming kin." The term she uses, *go'el*, links their circumstances to the levirate law, a law that will become pivotal in Ruth's tale. It is an injunction, laid out in Deuteronomy (25:5–6), that if a married man dies without children, it is the duty of a brother of the deceased to marry the widow, and the son of the union is considered to be the son of the first husband. The law is meant to preserve continuity, to prevent the devastating disaster of a family tree cut off, and, more implicitly, to ensure that support is given to childless widows. In the book of Ruth, the law is slightly modified, made applicable not only to the brothers of the deceased but also to his close relatives. Naomi does not spell out her wish, but she surely hints that Boaz may be able to offer more than barley if he would only venture to fulfill his obligation as a redeemer by marrying Ruth.

Ruth carries on with her gleaning until the barley harvest

and the wheat harvest are finished. She continues to be the hardworking migrant she was at the beginning of the harvest. But the question of whether Ruth will continue to be a poor gleaner or will instead be accepted into Boaz's household remains open. Boaz, for now, refrains from acknowledging his familial ties to the Moabite gleaner. But Ruth and Naomi cannot wait much longer. The harvest season is over, and the danger of hunger hovers once again in the air. A new plan must be concocted, and the threshing floor, where the winnowing of the grain is carried out after the harvest, seems to be the perfect site for it.

MIDNIGHT SEDUCTION ON THE THRESHING FLOOR:

THE SHADOW OF SODOM

The most enigmatic episode in Ruth's life takes place on the night in which she ventures to go down to the threshing floor, where Boaz sleeps. Landowners apparently slept on their threshing floors to guard their crops and take part in feasts that were held during the concluding stage of the harvest season. The idea that Ruth should sneak onto the threshing floor at night and approach the stack of barley where Boaz was lying is Naomi's:

> My daughter, shall I not seek for you a settled place for you, that it will be well for you? And now, is not Boaz our kinsman . . . at the threshing floor tonight? And you must bathe and anoint yourself and put on your garments and go down to the threshing floor. Do not let yourself be known to the man till he has finished eating and drinking. And it will be, when he lies down, that you will know the place where he lies down, and you shall come and uncover his feet and lie down, and as for him, he shall tell you what you should do. (3:1–4)

Naomi opens with a rhetorical question, expressing her maternal concern that her daughter-in-law has not yet found a husband, or—to use her curious, indirect term for marital life—a "settled place" (*manoach*). Without saying so explicitly, Naomi singles out Boaz as the preferred possibility and lays out her scheme. Ruth must bathe and anoint herself with perfumed oil, wear her finest garments, and then head to the threshing floor. On reaching the site, she should wait until Boaz has finished eating and drinking (wine, presumably) before lying down next to him. Naomi is undoubtedly staging a seduction scene. Even more striking, she stages a scene that bears an uncanny resemblance to the story of the dubious seduction of Lot by his daughters (one of whom is the foremother of Moab) at the cave near Sodom. The spirit of Sodom lurks behind the threshing floor of the book of Ruth.

The story of Sodom begins with God's wrath at the city for its utter corruption. To give the Sodomites one more chance to prove him wrong, God sends two divine messengers disguised as human men to the city. Lot welcomes the two angels into his house, following the cherished rules of hospitality. But then the men of the city encircle Lot's house seeking to gang-rape the visitors. Sodom is doomed. God ends up raining "brimstone and fire" upon Sodom (Genesis 19:24). But a moment before the city is destroyed, the messengers urge Lot to flee with his wife and daughters. On escaping they are ordered to refrain from looking back. Despite the prohibition, Lot's wife looks back and is turned into a pillar of salt. The only survivors of Sodom are thus Lot and his two daughters. And although Lot is presented as the only righteous person in Sodom, he is unwittingly seduced by his daughters. The older daughter turns to the younger one, saying, "Our father is old, and there is no man on earth to come to bed with us like the way of all the earth. Come, let us give our father wine to drink and let us lie with him, so that we may keep alive seed from our father" (19:31–32). The episode in the cave is not as abominable as the sins committed in Sodom—the daughters, after all, are trying to preserve the familial line—

27

but it is a clear violation of incest laws, among the primary laws of the biblical world. The two sons who are born out of this incestuous bond are none other than the founding fathers of two of ancient Israel's notorious enemies: Amon and Moab. From an Israelite perspective, the origins of both nations are thus stamped with the despicable mark of incest. In the case of Moab, the blemish is even reflected in the name: *mo'av* (Moab) is linked via a pun to *me'av* (from father). Sodom's story is exemplary of the tendency—all too common to this day—to attribute detestable sexual conduct to other cultures. It is no coincidence that immigrants or members of minorities are far more likely to be accused of rape or promiscuity. Illicit sexual desires are only too easily denied and projected onto others.

What then should we make of these Sodomite shades in the threshing floor scene? Let us first consider some of the similarities: in both stories there is a scheme to preserve the familial line via a questionable seduction, and in both cases the man is trapped in a moment of vulnerability, after drinking wine and falling asleep.[15] The threshing floor scene colors Ruth's portrait in ambiguous hues and discloses a lingering suspicion toward the Moabite who migrated to Bethlehem. But there are also palpable differences between the two stories. Those differences begin with the setting itself: the story of Lot and his daughters takes place in a cave and as such is associated with the uncivilized world, whereas the seduction scene in the book of Ruth unfolds on the threshing floor, an integral part of agricultural life. That the initiative was put forth by Naomi, an Israelite woman, rather than by a Moabite also makes it more acceptable. Most important, Ruth, unlike her foremothers, does not attempt to seduce her father but rather a father figure (Boaz calls her "my daughter" but is speaking only figuratively). And despite the unmistakable erotic innuendoes of the nocturnal encounter, it contains no blatant sexuality. Teasingly, the verb *lie* appears time and again, but no sexual act is consummated. Ruth lies down by Boaz, who "lay down at the edge of the stack of barley" (3:7), but their lying in such intimate proximity, however erotic, does not designate a sexual act.[16]

What exactly happened between the two on this harvest night, we'll never know. The dreamy quality of the encounter makes it all the more nebulous. It is a night of blurred identities, both enchanting and unsettling. After Ruth "uncovers his feet" (the feet may serve as a euphemistic description of his entire lower body) and lies close by, Boaz wakes up: "And it happened at midnight that the man trembled and twisted round, and, look, a woman was lying at his feet. And he said: 'Who are you?'" (3:8–9).[17] Boaz, who was capable of "recognizing" the foreign Ruth in the fields at midday, fails to recognize her at midnight. Perhaps he is in the bewildering liminal zone between dream and reality, startled by the woman who emerged from the dark, seeming to be a figment of his wild imagination. Trembling, he cannot figure out whether the woman who has exposed his feet is a dangerous evil spirit or a mysterious, benevolent seducer.

Midnight is the hour when ghosts and demons roam about, but in the biblical text it is also a potent time for radical transformations. The greatest story of redemption, the Exodus, takes place at midnight (Exodus 11:4, 12:29). In the book of Ruth, as in Exodus, midnight is, among other things, a redemptive moment: in this case, in an individual or familial sphere. In responding to the perplexed Boaz, Ruth identifies herself and calls for action: "I am Ruth your servant. May you spread your wing over your servant, for you are a redeeming kinsman [go'el]" (3:9). She has already taken a risk by sneaking onto the threshing floor at night; now she does not hesitate to take another gamble by audaciously adjuring Boaz to fulfill his responsibility. Rather than wait to hear what Boaz will tell her to do (as Naomi instructed her), she preserves her agency and defies gender norms.[18] Her rhetoric is brilliant, as usual. Echoing Boaz's

words in their first encounter in the field—"May the Lord requite your actions and may your reward be complete from the
Lord God of Israel under Whose wings [*kenafav*] you have
come to shelter" (2:12)—she now calls upon him to imitate God
in "spreading" his own wing over her. She does not speak explicitly of marriage, but the expression "to find shelter under
the wings of" is, among other things, a metaphor for marriage.
Ezekiel goes so far as to envision the covenantal marriage of
God and Israel in the wilderness after the Exodus via this metaphor: "And I passed by you and saw you, and, look, your time
was the time for lovemaking. And I spread My wing [*kenafi*]
over you and covered your nakedness, and vowed to you and
entered a covenant with you" (Ezekiel 16:8).[19] In assuming the
role of go'el, Ruth intimates, Boaz could follow the model of
the divine redeemer.

As Ruth stages her own seduction scene on the threshing
floor, she proves to be more acculturated than ever before,
knowing the ins and outs of the laws of her host country. Unlike her Moabite ancestor, Ruth does not violate the law. Quite
the contrary: she insists on the implementation of the levirate
law, on rescuing an endangered family tree in legal ways. But if
there is something magical about this night, it is because more
than justice and survival are at stake. Ruth and Boaz seem to
have been fond of each other from their first flirtatious encounter in the field.

Boaz cannot but yield to Ruth's daring marriage proposal,
but he does so with an unexpected twist. Instead of presenting
his yielding to Ruth's request as a hesed on his behalf, or an act
of charity, Boaz conveys his deep appreciation for her own hesed:
"Blessed are you to the Lord, my daughter, you have done better in your later kindness [*hesed*] than in the first, not going after
the young men, whether poor or rich. And now, my daughter,
do not be afraid. Whatever you say I will do for you, for all my

people's town [*sha 'ar'ami*] knows that you are a woman of valor" (3:10–12).[20] In preferring an older man to a younger one, he indicates, she will rescue him no less than he will save her. The kindness Ruth exhibited in cleaving to Naomi is now followed (from his perspective) by an even greater kindness, reflected in her choice to cling to him. He promises to do whatever she says and hails her as one who is considered by all the town's inhabitants—literally, "the gate of my people" (*sha 'ar'ami*)— as a "woman of valor" (*eshet hayil*). The migrant gleaner is thus admitted at midnight through the symbolic gate of the people as a worthy member of the community.

Although Boaz is eager to be a go'el at this instant, he is quick to point out a potential complication. Apparently there is a redeemer-kin who is closer in relation to Ruth's deceased husband. "Spend the night here," Boaz goes on to say, "and it shall be in the morning, should he redeem you, he will do well to redeem, and if he does not want to redeem you, I myself will redeem you, as the Lord lives" (3:13–14). Boaz presents the potential obstacle of a rival redeeming kin. But if he is not that worried, it is not only because he wants Ruth to spend the night on the threshing floor with him but also because he can well assume that the rival go'el will, in all likelihood, not be interested. The levirate law is not a law that is followed easily: it is a forced marriage that disrupts the familial lives of those who are required to implement it.[21] Redeeming a foreign widow only adds difficulties to the procedure.

Ruth leaves the threshing floor at the crack of dawn, at that liminal time in which nothing is discernable: "And she lay at his feet till morning and arose before a man could recognize his fellow man" (3:14). To be sure, she needs to protect her reputation, but the account of her departure also adds to the dreamy, mysterious quality of the scene and to the dark charm of their secretive flirtation bordering on impropriety. A moment before

Ruth departs, Boaz fills her shawl (*mitpahat*) with "six shares of barley"—a token of the clandestine bond that has been created between them and a promise of future plenitude and fertility.

Stealthily returning to her mother-in-law, Ruth is greeted with a question: *mi 'at*, "Who are you?" (3:16). Naomi probably means "How is it with you?" But strangely enough, her question is a verbatim repetition of the question that Boaz had asked earlier on the threshing floor when he woke up startled. Already in her instructions to Ruth in the opening of the chapter, Naomi is vicariously involved in all the details of the seduction scene, but here too, on asking "mi 'at," she sounds as if she were on the threshing floor. Naomi, who in the opening episode painfully imagines acquiring a husband "this very night" (1:12), only to reject the hope of a new beginning, is now granted the fulfillment of her dream via Ruth on another night. To make her mother-in-law feel all the more part of the experience, Ruth tells her about Boaz's benevolence and points to the profuse bounty of barley in her shawl: "These six shares of barley he gave me, for he said, 'You should not come empty-handed [*reikam*] to your mother-in-law'" (3:17). Boaz never mentions Naomi when he bestows the grain, but Ruth invents this detail in order to draw Naomi closer into the scene. Her words, however, also hark back to Naomi's bitter cry on entering Bethlehem: "I went out full, and empty [*reikam*] did the Lord bring me back" (1:21). On arriving at Bethlehem Naomi ignores the fact that she did not return "empty," for Ruth stood by her side; now she is indirectly called upon to acknowledge the fullness her Moabite daughter-in-law has introduced into her life. Naomi's sense of inner estrangement is somewhat alleviated, and Bethlehem, whose grain fills her belly beyond her wildest dreams, seems to be more of a home. With a growing capacity to believe in change, Naomi confidently remarks that Boaz will "not rest if he does not settle the matter today" (3:18). Now it is Boaz's turn to gamble.

AT THE GATE OF THE LAW:
INTERMARRIAGE AND MOTHERHOOD

Intermarriage is the migrant's royal road to acculturation, to becoming more visibly, more intimately part of the host culture. Ruth was already married to an Israelite in Moab, but when she moves to Bethlehem a different kind of intermarriage is at stake: one with an Israelite who lives in his homeland. Marriage seems to be the primary means of acculturation for migrant women, but not the exclusive one. It is at times part of the tales of migrant men as well. When Joseph becomes Pharaoh's top adviser and passes for an Egyptian, he marries Asenath, the daughter of an Egyptian priest. And Moses's marriage to Zipporah, who is also a daughter of a priest (Jethro), is vital to his acceptance within Midianite culture. Ruth, much like Joseph and Moses, does not simply marry a "local"; she marries a local of high standing. The possibility of marrying Boaz would completely alter the trajectory of Ruth's life, securing her membership in Bethlehem while providing an immediate entrance into the realm of the town's leading elite.

The fourth and final chapter of the book of Ruth begins with a scene at the gate, the principal public place of the town, where courts of justice are run by affluent elders. Wasting no time (as Naomi has predicted), Boaz goes the following morning to the gate to settle the legal matters that would make his matrimonial bond with Ruth possible. If during their nocturnal encounter Boaz praises Ruth for being considered by the "gate of his people" as a "woman of valor," now he sits at the literal gate of his people to make Ruth's entrance into the Israelite community of Bethlehem official. His expectation that the redeemer-kin is likely to pass by this central location proves correct. On seeing the potential go'el approaching, Boaz calls to him and says, "Turn aside, sit down here, So-and-so" (4:1). The name of the closer kin is not even mentioned. He is referred to as *ploni almoni*, "So-and-so," marking him from the outset as one whose role in the plot will turn out to be marginal. Boaz's social stature is apparent not only in his handling of So-and-so but also in the ease with which he "takes" ten men of the town elders to serve as witnesses.

An intricate legal drama then unfolds at the gate. The savvy Boaz does not raise the issue of the levirate law immediately. Instead, he opens with the need to redeem Naomi's field. Apparently Naomi inherited a parcel of Elimelech's land (a rare case of a childless widow who is granted the right to own land), but because of her impoverishment, she was forced to sell it. According to Leviticus 25:24–25, land must be preserved within the familial domain and "redeemed"—that is, bought back—in cases in which a family member is forced to sell. To Boaz's question of whether he would be willing to redeem Naomi's land, So-and-so says yes. But then, in an unexpected swerve, Boaz clarifies that the law of redemption and the levirate law are inextricably connected: "On the day you acquire the field from Naomi, you will also acquire Ruth the Moabite to raise up the name of the dead on his estate" (4:5). The word *redeem* is primarily used in the biblical legal corpus in relation to land redemption. In the book of Ruth, however, it is also used to designate levirate marriage, which is why Boaz can more easily combine the two laws.[22]

So-and-so hastens to withdraw, worried that such a marriage would "spoil [his] estate." He leaves unstated why this is so, but what seems to bother him is Ruth's Moabite origin. Deuteronomy 23:4 prohibits marriage to Ammonites and Moabites because they showed no mercy to the wandering Israelites on their way to the Promised Land. The authors of the book of Ruth were either unaware of this law or opposed to it. Intermarriage with Ruth is nowhere regarded as a legal violation; in fact, it is a legal obligation. And yet the story of Sodom, we may assume, suffices to generate trepidation. So-and-so is the male counterpart of Orpah. He is not a sinner, but he is more conventional in his choices and as such serves as a foil to highlight the exceptional courage of Boaz.

In assuming the role of redeemer, Boaz makes sure to acquire the land while marrying Ruth. This double transaction underscores the fact that his marriage to Ruth is by extension meant to redeem Naomi as well. Much as Naomi's spirit hovered over the threshing floor, so now she becomes an integral part of the legal deal at the gate. Even potentially tense situations are resolved without conflict in the book of Ruth. So-and-so acquiesces and passes on the right of redemption to Boaz. And Boaz, in turn, announces before the eyes of the elders and the people who gather there, "You are witnesses today that I have acquired all that was Elimelech's and all that was Chilion's and Mahlon's from the hand of Naomi. And also Ruth the Moabite, wife of Mahlon, I have acquired for myself as wife, to raise up the name of the dead on his estate, that the name of the dead be not cut off from his brothers and from the gate of his place" (4:9–10). Ruth is redeemed and so is the land. The most dreaded scenario of the deceased being cut off from "the gate of his place" (sha'ar mekomo) is prevented.

We do not know whether Ruth now enters the scene and stands by Boaz at the gate, but the elders deliver a testimony and a blessing that could have been part of a wedding ceremony. Once again we have a brief poetic inset—a few parallelisms—this time in order to highlight the celebratory quality of the moment:

And all the people who were in the gate and the elders said, "We are witnesses. May the LORD make the woman coming into your house like Rachel and like Leah, both of whom built the house of Israel. . . . And may your house be like the house of Perez to whom Tamar gave birth by Judah, from the seed that this young woman will give you." (4:11–12)

As Ruth is welcomed into Boaz's household, she is linked to a whole genealogy of formidable women, from the founding matriarchs, Rachel and Leah, to Tamar, the foremother of the house of Perez.

The elders' blessing is not only future oriented. In the various scenes that precede the ceremony at the gate, Ruth's actions are already cast, if implicitly, in relation to those of the three founding female figures of Genesis. Yet the majestic quality of the elders' blessing mitigates the complexities of the evocation of this female lineage. However distinguished these three women of the past may be, they are all involved in questionable transactions and seductions. To begin with Rachel and Leah, the most pertinent story is that of the mandrakes. The two sisters, as one recalls, are both married to Jacob and forever engaged in quarrels. Their rivalry is especially harsh because each of them longs for something the other has. While Leah, the older sister, bears sons one after the other, Rachel, the younger one, is barren. And whereas Rachel is from the outset Jacob's true beloved, Leah is the neglected wife who never stops yearning for the love she is denied. Mutual despair eventually leads the two to strike a deal. Rachel offers Jacob for a night (Jacob is put in the humiliating position of being a token of exchange between the two women), while Leah gives her sister mandrakes, the fruit which promises fertility. Under God's auspices, both sisters become pregnant, although Leah gives birth first, perhaps as an implied criticism of Rachel's willingness to use dubious means to acquire fertility.[23]

The story of Tamar is another poignant case of a questionable sexual scene. Its relevance to Ruth's tale is even more apparent given that it revolves around the implementation of the levirate law. Tamar is Judah's daughter-in-law, the wife of Er, his firstborn. After Er dies, Judah demands that Onan, his second son, marry Tamar in order "to raise up seed" (Genesis 38:8) for his brother. Onan obeys his father, but whenever he comes to bed with Tamar, he makes sure to "waste his seed on the ground" (38:9). Knowing that the child he would beget with Tamar would not be his own but rather his deceased brother's, he is reluctant to be a surrogate father. God is enraged and puts Onan to death. Judah is now obligated to promise Tamar that she will be given to his youngest son, Shelah, when he grows older. But a long time passes and Judah fails to keep his promise. The plot thickens when Tamar decides to take action rather than wait passively. She takes off her widow's garb and covers herself with a veil and sits by the entrance of Enaim, waiting for Judah to pass by. Taking her for a whore, Judah asks to lie with her and provides his seal-and-cord and staff as a pledge that he will send a kid from his flock as payment. Later, Judah hears that his daughter-in-law "conceived by her whoring" (38:24). Without thinking twice, he sentences her to death: "Take her out to be burned" (38:24). Tamar does not remain silent, however, and turns to her father-in-law, saying, "By the man to whom those belong I have conceived. . . . Recognize, pray, whose are this seal-and-cord and this staff?" Judah recognizes them and has the courage to admit that he has wronged her: "She is more in the right than I [*tsadka mimeni*], for have I not failed to give her to Shelah, my son?" (38:25–26). Tamar ends up giving birth to twins: Perez—none other than Boaz's ancestor—and Zerah.

Embracing Ruth as a member of the community at the town gate entails, wittingly or unwittingly, an acknowledgment that the house of Israel was from the very outset "built" through semi-transgressive acts that turn out to be far more beneficial than one would expect. Much as the dubious deal of Rachel and Leah ultimately leads to the birth of some of the founding fathers of the Israelite tribes, and much as Tamar's ruse results in the birth of Perez, the great-grandfather of Boaz and the progenitor of the Davidic dynasty, so too the scheming of Ruth and Naomi paves the way to the birth of the future leaders of the nation. We should note, however, that although Ruth is regarded as a founding matriarch by the elders, she is still called "Ruth the Moabite" in the following verse (4:13). The continuous marking of Ruth's foreignness calls attention to the limits of her acculturation. She is part of Israelite culture, present at its very core, yet something of a stranger.

The narrative moves swiftly from a description of the ceremony at the gate to a brief comment on Ruth's pregnancy and the birth of a son, Obed. The much sought-after child now enters the scene. And although Naomi remains childless—the miracle of giving birth in old age is granted only to Sarah—she too becomes a mother of sorts in assuming the role of Obed's caregiver: "And Naomi took the child and placed him in her lap and became a nurse for him" (4:16). In previous episodes, Ruth shares the barley with her mother-in-law; at this concluding scene, she shares mothering. She could have added to her oath yet another statement: "My son is your son." In Ruth's version of the levirate law, redeeming is not only a means to preserve the memory of Mahlon but also, and perhaps even more so, a way of rescuing Naomi from the pits of life. This shared motherhood is supported by the law: given that Obed is considered to be Mahlon's son, Naomi is actually his grandmother.

It seems like a remarkably blissful moment, a happy ending to a tale that began with migration, childlessness, and widowhood. We noted Toni Morrison's comments about contemporary literature's suspicion of goodness. We could say the same about a certain modern distrust of hope. Reading this ancient tale allows us to rethink our current inclinations. In its intricate endorsement of hesed and perseverance in impossible conditions, Ruth's tale teaches us the value of devoting attention to these admirable human potentialities. Nobody lives "happily ever after," and the agonies of the past do not vanish, but the joys of a new home and the hope for a better future loom large.

What makes this ending less of a happy ending from today's

perspective, however, is that Ruth and Naomi do not utter a word throughout it. We may well wonder why. Are they marginalized now that the primary problem of rescuing the familial line has been resolved? The special attention given to women's agency throughout the tale diminishes considerably once we enter the male zone of the gate—but not entirely. There is yet one more voice that offers an unexpected perspective.

Out of the blue, the collective voice of the women neighbors emerges. They too, like the elders, insert celebratory poetic clauses in their blessing. Addressing Naomi, they declare, "Blessed is the Lord, Who has not deprived you of a redeemer today. . . . And may he be a restorer of life for you and a support for your old age, as your daughter-in-law, who loves you, has borne him, who has been better to you than seven sons" (4:14–15).[24] The women neighbors may be reflecting Naomi's own sense of elation at witnessing the gradual restoration of her world via the birth of her grandson, the "restorer of life." But they may also be filling the void of a happiness she cannot fully experience, given the lingering presence of her losses and dislocations. Their words are not only soothing but unexpectedly radical. The women go so far as to define Ruth as "better to [Naomi] than seven sons"! This is an astonishing acknowledgment of Ruth's merit in a world where the birth of sons is a primary objective. The women neighbors may also be trying to encourage Naomi to relinquish any trace of ambivalence she might still harbor vis-à-vis her Moabite daughter-in-law. But the book of Ruth does not end with this homage to Ruth.

The final note of the book of Ruth is devoted to a genealogy: "And this is the lineage of Perez. Perez begat Hezron. And Hezron begat Ram and Ram begat Aminadab. And Aminadab begat Nahshon, and Nahshon begat Salmah. And Salmah begat Boaz, and Boaz begat Obed. And Obed begat Jesse, and Jesse begat David" (4:18–22). In its emulation of the genealogies of Genesis, this genealogy captures the beat of life over the chasm of time, the steady emergence of each generation following the previous one. Genealogies, among other things, are humanity's response to death. In each "begat" phrase, we are reminded that the clan, the community continues to survive. That Mahlon's name does not appear in this genealogy is understandable. His name is akin to "illness," and although it proved to be prophetic (like that of his brother Chilion, "destruction"), it is too somber to be included in the family tree.[25] Despite the guidelines of the levirate law, it is Boaz who is presented as Obed's father; the name of the deceased is resurrected only implicitly.

There is, however, another glaring omission. The closing genealogy (like all other biblical genealogies) omits the women who played an essential role in making this lineage possible. We move from fathers to sons with no mention of the mothers who birthed them. Is this an attempt to downplay the exceptional emphasis on women's lives in the book of Ruth? Should this ending be seen as analogous to the ending of Ecclesiastes, whose penultimate verse—"fear God and keep His commands, for that is all humankind" (12:13)—is unmistakably incongruous with the heretical teachings of Qohelet? But as is the case with Ecclesiastes, the final words of the book of Ruth cannot efface that which preceded them.

The last member of the concluding genealogy is David. We now realize that Ruth's deeds were vital not only to the survival of Elimelech's clan but also to the very foundation of the cherished Israelite dynasty. Ruth's affiliation with David, we may assume, facilitated her entry into the canon, adding a royal stamp to that of the elders at the gate. But the link to the Davidic dynasty is by no means the only factor that paved Ruth's way to Holy Writ. Whether consciously or not, whether willingly or despite themselves, the canon makers were keen on preserving some oddities in the biblical corpus. Alongside the book of Ruth are other distinct anomalies in the biblical text, among them books such as Ecclesiastes, Job, and the Song of Songs, whose inclusion in the canon is a cause for wonder. What seems to have contributed to the tipping of the scales in favor of these anomalous texts is the exquisite literary power with which they present views that run against the grain. That the canon makers would not have used such terms to justify their choice does not make aesthetic considerations less pertinent. We can imagine that Ruth's tale of migration was in no small part canonized because no one could resist this literary gem—there was something utterly compelling about its call that we recognize what we might gain by taking an unfamiliar path, by seeing the world from the perspective of a migrant Moabite woman.

The biblical rendition of Ruth's life ends with her marriage to Boaz and her giving birth to Obed. What happened to her in the ensuing years is nowhere disclosed. We do not know how she felt on becoming part of Boaz's household, whether she continued to take care of Naomi, if she ever had additional children, or if she ever woke up at night with longings for Moab, wondering what would have happened had she chosen to return to her mother's house. In the portraits of prominent male figures in the Bible such as Jacob and David, we receive detailed stories of their decline in old age and their struggles to determine their heirs. No such account is available in the book of Ruth, nor is Ruth ever mentioned in any other biblical text. And yet, Ruth's story does not end with the concluding chapter of her book. She springs back to life, repeatedly revived and reimagined, in an array of captivating afterlives from late antiquity to today.

2

◆◦◆◦◆

The Convert

RUTH RESURFACES in Late Antiquity as a convert. Once conversion becomes part of Jewish tradition and law in the rabbinic world of Late Antiquity, Ruth is regarded as a notable precursor and is set on a pedestal as one whose story can serve as a model for potential converts. In fact, ever since the rabbis positioned Ruth as an exemplary convert, she has often been cherished as such. Even today many women who convert to Judaism choose "Ruth" as their Hebrew name.

Many assume that Ruth was designated as a convert already in the Bible, but this is not the case. Within the biblical world, the concept of conversion does not exist. The term *ger*, as we have seen, refers to strangers, or sojourners, who have become part of the Israelite community. The ger must follow some of the basic Mosaic laws and is granted certain rights (among them the right to glean) but is not required to officially become an Israelite. For the rabbis, however, the biblical demarcations between Israelites and foreign residents were too fluid. They sought to draw clearer distinctions between Jews and non-Jews and to regulate the entrance of newcomers.[1] The term *ger* is still used in the rabbinic context, but it becomes the designation for a convert. And as the ger becomes a convert new laws are formed: *hilkhot gerim*, the laws of conversion. Potential converts are required to prove their unconditional willingness to convert, study the commandments, and undergo ritual immersion as well as circumcision (in the case of men) if they wish to become part of the Jewish community.

Conversion emerges as rabbinic Judaism strives to distinguish itself from other religions in Roman Palestine. The Jewish community lived under Roman rule, and it continually struggled against the lure of a well-established pagan culture. The rise of Christianity and its increasing popularity were additional causes for concern. In reflecting on conversion and establishing the laws governing it, the rabbis did not only provide criteria for the acceptance of new members; they sought to redefine the contours of Judaism against the competing precepts and practices of their Roman and Christian rivals.[2] This is indeed what makes conversion so fascinating: it is a social phenomenon that encapsulates the most cherished principles of a given religion. The rabbis, however, did not present us with a unified version of Jewish conversion and, by extension, of Judaism as a whole. Rabbinic culture—and this is its most renowned feature—is above all else a culture of debate, which is why we receive multiple perspectives, even conflicting ones, on conversion and converts.

The predominant rabbinic tendency is to embrace converts. Relying on Deuteronomy 10:18, where God is defined as one who loves gerim and cares for their needs, the rabbis deduce that the convert holds a unique position before the divine king: "Now who is greater," they ask, "he who loves the king or he whom the king loves?"[3] Similarly, the great Talmudic sage Resh

Lakish claims that the convert is "more precious in the sight of the Holy One, blessed be He, than those who stood at the foot of Sinai. Why is this so? If those who stood at the foot of Mount Sinai had not experienced the thunder, the flames, the lightning, the quaking of the mountain, and the sound of the shofarot, they would not have accepted the yoke of the Kingdom of Heaven upon themselves, whereas the proselyte, who witnessed none of these things, makes himself acceptable to the Holy One, blessed be He, and receives upon himself the yoke of the Kingdom of Heaven. Is there anyone more precious than this?"[4] Though less prevalent, disapproving perspectives on converts also appear in the rabbinic corpus, the most notorious being that "converts are as difficult for Israel as a scab" (*sapahat*).[5]

But the major debate among the rabbis was not about whether to accept converts but whether to be lenient or stringent toward them. One of the disputations between Shammai and Hillel, the two famous rival sages, revolves around the proper treatment of those who wish to convert. A memorable tale captures the contours of the controversy. A gentile who aspires to convert approaches Shammai and says, "Convert me and teach me the entire Torah while I am standing on one foot." Shammai pushes him away with a builder's yardstick. Shammai does not believe in shortcuts; he refuses to make conversion easy by turning the required teachings into something that can be learned in no time, "while standing on one foot." When the same gentile comes before Hillel, the more lenient sage converts him on the spot, summing up Judaism via a single instruction: "What is hateful to you do not do to another; that is the whole Torah, and the rest is its interpretation. Go study."[6] Hillel follows his own ethical guideline in respecting the gentile's request. But he also urges him to use this one key imperative as an invitation to study further, beyond the moment of conversion. The spirits of both sages hover over Jewish conversion in the rabbinic world, a practice that is both strict and welcoming. Conversion is not meant to be easy in Judaism. There is no missionary goal to convert as many gentiles as possible. Quite the contrary—those who wish to join the Jewish people have to make an effort to do so, and the initiative must be theirs. But once they prove their determination to convert, they are accepted without reservation.

Ruth is singled out in rabbinic literature as one of the most distinguished converts from the "nations of the world" whom God himself brought to his people as a gift.[7] How did Ruth ascend to this privileged position? Primarily through her oath on the road, and especially her statement "Your people is my people, and your god is my god," which lends itself to a reading of Ruth as an ideal convert, righteous and pious in equal measure. Already in the biblical text, Ruth's vow to follow Naomi's God and people paves her way to Bethlehem, but in the rabbinic context it is seen as more than a broad commitment to embrace the host culture's precepts: it is a concrete indication of her eagerness to convert. What makes Ruth all the more fitting, in rabbinic eyes, is the fact that she commits herself to both Israel and its God. In doing so, she endorses, as it were, the dual character of Jewish conversion. Jewish converts, unlike Christian converts, not only adopt a different religious framework; they also commit themselves to a particular community. The rabbis would have had to invent Ruth if she were not already waiting for them among the biblical scrolls.

While most rabbis chose to extol Ruth's merit, we also find commentaries that reflect negative rabbinic views on converts. In these cases, the intimations of ambivalence in the biblical text vis-à-vis Ruth's Moabite origin are intensified and used as a springboard to undermine the validity of her conversion.

The most extensive and prominent compilation of rabbinic commentaries, or midrashim, on the book of Ruth is Ruth Rabbah.[8] It was composed in the period of the Amoraic sages (220–500 CE), but its final editing took place much later, presumably around the eighth century.[9] Midrashic exegesis of the book of Ruth—and this is true of midrashic hermeneutics altogether—provides not an interpretation of the text as a whole but rather a verse-by-verse commentary. From the rabbis' perspective, every verse (or almost every verse) of the book of Ruth requires utmost attention, every lacuna needs to be probed. And given that this midrashic corpus is a composite text, offering a patchwork of sources from distinct periods, we receive at times a plethora of diverse commentaries on the same episode, some attributed to specific sages while others remain anonymous.

The midrashic corpus on the book of Ruth (like every other midrashic collection) was composed within the domain of one of the central institutions of rabbinic Judaism: the *beit midrash*, the rabbinic house of study, where biblical texts were studied and expounded. Women were barred from entering this distinctly male exegetical sphere. But as Galit Hasan-Rokem points out, the boundaries between the beit midrash and the home, the quintessential space of women, were more pliable than we might expect.[10] Within the midrashic world, we find brief tales about women who yearned to take part in exegetical endeavors. We hear of a nameless woman who used to sit and listen to Rabbi Meir's teachings, though her unconventional conduct led to marital problems (her husband was furious that she devoted so much attention to Rabbi Meir). And we are told that Bruriah, the daughter of Rabbi Hananiah ben Teradion, ventured to engage in exegetical debates with several rabbis and was greatly admired for her breadth of knowledge. These are but textual traces, but they may be representative of a broader, unrecorded phenomenon.

In carving out their Ruth, the rabbis were more often than not determined to cast her in traditional feminine roles. On occasion, however, they ventured to translate the agency allotted to Ruth in the biblical text into their own terms. In doing so, the rabbis may have been influenced by the exceptional women who were drawn to the exegetical world of the beit midrash. Or perhaps they were attuned to the women's lore that they heard in their own homes. Or perhaps they were interested in exploring, at least in their exegetical imagination, a wider range of potential gender roles.

CONVERSION ON THE ROAD

The first image that we receive of Ruth in Ruth Rabbah is that of a princess. Ruth is envisioned as the daughter of Eglon, king of Moab (Ruth Rabbah 2:9).[11] The rabbis set out to fill in the biblical lacuna regarding Ruth's Moabite background, but they are rather terse, providing no details about her life at the palace. Midrashic commentaries on biblical texts are usually short and compact, but in this case they are particularly brief because the rabbis are far more interested in the subsequent episodes of Ruth's life—the period when she becomes a convert and her real path to glory begins.

Where does Ruth's conversion take place? As far as the rabbis are concerned, this momentous event occurs on the road between Moab and Bethlehem, though the interpretations vary. Pivotal moments in the book of Ruth generate a profusion of midrashic responses. Ruth's oath is among them. According to Samuel ben Nahmani, the process of conversion began with Naomi's recurrent plea that her daughters-in-law turn back and return to Moab (Ruth 1:8): "Three times it is written 'turn back,' corresponding to the three times that a would-be convert is rejected; but if he persists, he is accepted. . . . A man should rebuff with his left hand, but bring near with the right" (Ruth Rabbah 2.16).[12] Samuel ben Nahmani traces a scene of conversion in this preliminary exchange, viewing Naomi as following the rabbinic practice of initially pushing away would-be converts to test their degree of commitment. He does not spell out the rest of the scene, but the implication is clear: we are meant to infer that because Orpah turns back, she is unworthy of conversion, whereas Ruth, who stays with Naomi and vows to accept her mother-in-law's God and people, is precisely the kind of convert who should be ultimately brought near with the right hand.[13]

The most elaborate accounts of Ruth's conversion focus on her oath. In an anonymous commentary on this scene, Ruth and Naomi are imagined as engaged in a conversation on hilkhot gerim, the laws of conversion (what else?), as they walk along the road. In fact, Ruth's passionate declaration of loyalty is construed as a series of responses to Naomi's introduction of hilkhot gerim.

> *And Ruth said: "Do not entreat me to forsake you, to turn back from you"* [Ruth 1:16]. What is the meaning of *"do not entreat me"*? She said to her, ". . . I am fully determined to convert, but it is better that it would be by you than by another." When Naomi heard this, she began to teach her the laws of conversion, saying: "My daughter, it is not the custom of daughters of Israel to go to gentile theaters and circuses," to which she replied, *"For wherever you go, I will go."* She proceeded: "My daughter, it is not the custom of daughters of Israel to dwell in a house with no *mezuzah*," to which she responded, *"And where you lodge, I will lodge." "Your people is my people"* refers to the penalties and admonitions [of the Torah], and *"your God is my God"* to the other commandments. (Ruth Rabbah 2:22)

Acknowledging the unusual agency of Ruth and Naomi in the biblical text, the Midrash casts them in the prominent roles of a wise instructor and her formidable student. These are definitely not typical female roles in rabbinic culture. The rabbis may have been inspired by the few women of their community who were familiar with legal, halachic matters. But whether or not contemporary women were on their minds, they did not hesitate to position two biblical women in this elevated position. In response to Ruth's unwavering request to be converted, Naomi sets out to instruct her, presenting some of the customs of the Jewish faith, highlighting their demanding character. She tries at first to dissuade her daughter-in-law, but Ruth is not deterred by the list of prohibitions and remains determined to convert. The midrashic Ruth is as resolved as the biblical Ruth, but her motivation is strikingly different. In Ruth Rabbah, Ruth does not cling to the God and the people of Israel as a token of her hesed toward Naomi but rather because she is inherently drawn to the Israelite faith and is keen on adopting it "under any circumstances." Conversion for the sake of human love, marriage, or material gain is unacceptable from a rabbinic perspective. The only legitimate conversion is carried out for the sake of heaven.[14]

Naomi's instructions highlight exigencies that would be particularly pertinent to a woman convert. She indicates that the daughters of Israel are chaste, which is why they would never consider attending what in Jewish eyes are the embodiments of the promiscuous world of the Romans: theaters and circuses. A common practice of Roman imperial culture—the remains of spacious theaters in Caesarea and Beth She'an are proof of the centrality of such edifices in Roman Palestine as well—is thus projected back on to biblical times. The midrashic Ruth, however, is not bothered by this historical imprecision and adopts Naomi's guidelines wholeheartedly. In declaring "For wherever you go, I will go," she presumably vows to keep Israelite customs and avoid attending the despicable entertainment sites of the pagans. The next item on Naomi's list is the mezuzah, the scroll attached to the doorpost of Jewish homes in obedience to Deuteronomy 6:4–9. The biblical verses that need to be inscribed on the mezuzah are those taken from Deuteronomy, beginning with the renowned phrase "Hear, Israel [*shema Yisrael*], the Lord our God, the Lord is one." Placing a mezuzah on the door of one's abode is an essential mark of Jewish identity and, according to the rabbis, one of the 613 mitzvot (commandments). To be sure, this commandment is not meant solely for "the daughters of Israel," but Naomi presents it as especially relevant to women, intimating that the domestic sphere is primarily a feminine realm. Once again the midrashic Ruth accepts her mother-in-law's teaching and declares that she will lodge only where Naomi lodges and refrain from dwelling in a house without a mezuzah. From the theaters and circuses to the Jewish home, Naomi charts the rabbis' spatial parameters for Jewish women who wish to abide by the law.

To be converted, writes the philosopher William James, means "to be regenerated, to receive grace, to experience religion, to gain an assurance"; it means to undergo a process "gradual or sudden, by which a self, hitherto divided, and consciously wrong, inferior and unhappy, becomes unified and consciously right . . . in consequence of its firmer hold upon religious realities."[15] James's definition is pertinent to stories of conversion in the Christian world from Saint Augustine to Saint Teresa, but it does not apply to the rabbinic configuration of conversion. Rather than focusing on an inner experience, the rabbis are concerned with legal issues. Their preoccupation, however, is not as technical as it might seem. It is through the law that religion and community—the two axes of Jewish conversion—intersect, and major theological concepts are interwoven within the webs of communal life. In highlighting Ruth's unconditional willingness to follow the commandments and accept the everyday practices of Jewish communities, the Midrash thus bolsters her position as an exemplary Jewish convert.

Ruth's conversion is not merely compatible with rabbinic precepts, her tale is the very ground upon which some of these precepts were founded. The conversation between Ruth and Naomi on the laws of conversion in Ruth Rabbah is the inspiration for the rather tough admission ritual of a potential convert in tractate Yevamot in the Babylonian Talmud: "A (potential) convert who approaches to be converted, they say to him:

'Why have you decided to approach (us) to be converted? Do you know that Israel[ites] at this time are pained, oppressed, harassed, and torn, and that afflictions come upon them?' If he says 'I know and am unworthy,' they accept him immediately. And they make known to him a few of the light commandments and a few of the severe commandments" (BT Yevamot 47a–b).[16] In Yevamot, the potential convert, much like Ruth, is encouraged not to convert. Why would anyone want to follow the demanding legal corpus of a people who are, more often than not, pained and oppressed? But here too, conversion ultimately takes place owing to the persistence of the candidate. The candidate is required not only to indicate that he is well aware of what awaits him but also to acknowledge his humble position. In saying "I know and am unworthy," the potential convert makes clear that he in no way assumes that he deserves to be accepted by this persecuted people.[17] It is only then that they pass on to him details about some of the required commandments. Note that the potential convert in the Talmud is male, which is why the more specific commandments that are highlighted are different.

Among the central prohibitions that appear in Yevamot are those related to dietary restrictions (eating forbidden fat) and keeping the Sabbath. More curious is the demand to refrain from violating the laws of gleaning, the forgotten sheaf, the corner of the field, and the poor tithe. This list of biblical laws, whose primary purpose is to ensure basic rights to the poor, may have been meant as a warning not to abuse the Jewish welfare system and convert only in order to gain social benefits. But could it also be an implicit homage to Ruth? Perhaps the rabbis, who gleaned in Ruth's field while shaping the contours of Jewish conversion, were keen on highlighting the great value of the laws that were indispensable in the life of the ancient gleaner.

According to another anonymous commentary, Ruth's oath

encapsulates not a discussion about hilkhot gerim but rather a record of a conversion ritual that unfolds through a journey to different sites of Israelite worship: "'*For wherever you go, I will go*': to the tent of testimony, to Gilgal, Shiloh . . . and the Permanent Temple. '*And wherever you lodge I will lodge*': I will lodge with the sacrifices. '*Your people is my people,*' in that I will abolish the idolatry within me, and then '*your God is my God,*' the reward of my labor" (Ruth Rabbah 2:23). Ruth is a pilgrim who defies chronology. She travels in time to both the past and the future—from the tent of testimony (where worship was held during the wanderings in the wilderness) to the future Temple in the days of Solomon. And while attending the sacrifices at the Temple, she readily "destroys" the idolatry "within" her. This midrashic rendition of Ruth's conversion is more spiritual in its orientation, but even here the emphasis is on religious practices rather than a metaphysical experience, and here too, conversion is by no means imposed; it stems from Ruth's wholehearted desire to become part of the people of Israel and its history.

By the time Ruth and Naomi walk together toward Bethlehem, after Naomi finally realizes that Ruth is determined to join her (Ruth 1:18), the two women are seen as set on the same footing. "Come and see how precious in the eyes of the Omnipresent are converts," comments Rabbi Judah ben Simon: "Once she decided to convert, she is set on an equal footing with Naomi" (Ruth Rabbah 3:5). From Rabbi Judah ben Simon's perspective, Naomi's silent acknowledgment of her daughter-in-law's efforts to convert reflects God's own great love for and appreciation of true converts.

COMPLICATIONS: MOABITE WOMEN
AND THE QUESTION OF MODESTY

What complicates Ruth's story of conversion is the fact that she is not just a foreign woman but a Moabite woman. One of

the issues that trouble the rabbis is the prohibition of Deuteronomy 23:4. According to this prohibition, Ammonites and Moabites are not to be accepted into the Lord's assembly because
they did not greet the Israelites with bread and water on their
way to the Promised Land. The authors of the book of Ruth
were either unaware of this law or opposed to it, but the rabbis
could not ignore the prohibition and thus had to justify the fact
that a Moabite woman was allowed to convert and marry an
Israelite. What was their solution to this exegetical problem?
Women were exempt. The prevailing argument is summed up
in the following commentary: "Ammonite but not Ammoni-
tess, Moabite, but not Moabitess" (Ruth Rabbah 2:9). If the law
were meant to include women, it would have included a feminine noun, *moavit* (Moabitess), rather than only the masculine
moavi (Moabite). Masters of exegetical acrobatics, the rabbis
suspend their grammatical knowledge (they know only too well
that the singular masculine mode in biblical law is often used in
reference to both men and women), and insist, in this case, on
being hyperliteral.

But proving that Moabite women could be admitted to the
Lord's assembly is not always perceived as sufficient. Some rabbis seem determined to "de-Moabize" Ruth. They do so by ex-
tolling her as an emblem of modesty, innocent of the lewdness
that was often attributed to Moabite women.[18] The rabbis are
no advocates of multiculturalism. If they admire converts, it is
because true converts willingly eradicate any trace of their culture of origin. One of the midrashic strategies for glorifying
Ruth is to set Orpah as her wicked opposite. In the book of
Ruth itself, as we have seen, Orpah is not evil. Her only "crime"
is to be conventional in her choices. In the Midrash, however,
she becomes the dark double of her righteous sister-in-law: a
wanton, idolatrous woman who lies with no less than one hundred uncircumcised men on the very night on which she leaves
Naomi and heads back to Moab (Ruth Rabbah 2:20). No wonder

the midrashic Orpah ends up being the foremother of David's archenemy, Goliath.

Ruth's modesty continues to be a central theme in midrashic considerations of the ensuing scenes in the book of Ruth. Generally the rabbis opt to show that Ruth remained an impeccable convert in each and every episode of her life. Thus when the rabbis meditate on Ruth's work in the fields, they present her as an exceptionally modest gleaner: "All the other women flirt with the reapers while she recedes; all the other women gather from between the sheaves, while she gathers from that which is left over" (Ruth Rabbah 4:6). Much as Ruth adheres to the codes of gleaning and gathers only what is permissible, so too she abides by the mores of sexual propriety. Rather than exposing her body and flirting with the reapers, Ruth is restrained. She is superior not only to Moabite women, we discover, but to "all the other women," presumably even to the Israelite women of Bethlehem who glean in the fields.

To portray Ruth as a modest gleaner is a fairly easy task. What is far more difficult is to regard her deeds on the threshing floor as chaste. Well aware of the echoes of Sodom in this scene, the rabbis spell out what is only intimated in the biblical text: the somewhat disturbing similarity between the respective seductions by Ruth and Lot's daughters, one of whom is the foremother of Moab. But as they lay bare the ambivalence embedded in the biblical account, they also highlight the differences between the two tales. Whereas the "first impregnation [*ibbur*] of Moab," claim Rabbi Hanina the son of Papa and Rabbi Simon, "was not for the sake of Heaven" but "for the sake of whoredom" (*znut*), Ruth's motives on the threshing floor were worthy (Ruth Rabbah 5:14). To further underscore Ruth's merit, these rabbis add a reference to another story. They see the incestuous "impregnation" in the cave near Sodom as leading directly to the abomination in the plains of Moab, where the daughters of Moab lured the children of Israel "to go whoring" (they cite Numbers 25:1). This juggling of several biblical texts is definitely confusing, but finding interconnections in the Bible, as Daniel Boyarin has amply shown, is precisely one of the exegetical goals (and pleasures) of the rabbis.[19] Their assumption is that a verse is made rich in meaning through its links to other scriptural texts. Biblical verses are not fixed; they forever shift across multiple contexts and so create new understandings. The rabbis' links are at times totally fanciful, but they are often attuned to the incredibly intricate web of textual interconnections that are a central feature of biblical poetics. In this case, Rabbi Hanina and Rabbi Simon are close to the mark: the three tales that they bring together are indeed linked in the Bible. The two rabbis, however, erase some of the ambiguities in the book of Ruth in proposing that the more significant affinity is between Lot's daughters and the wanton daughters of Moab. Ruth's virtuous modesty, they claim, marks her as an admirable exception within a chain of interrelated episodes regarding Moabite women.

Again and again, the rabbis refuse to simply ignore the erotic, and potentially problematic, details of the threshing floor scene. Instead, their instinct is to push farther into the specifics, to delve into the details. The liveliest dramatization of the unsettling eroticism of this scene occurs in this midrash: "*And it happened at midnight that the man trembled and twisted round* [Ruth 3:8]. She gripped him like ivy, and he began to feel her hair. 'Spirits have no hair,' he thought, so he said: '*Who are you?*' [Ruth 3:9], a woman or a spirit?' She answered, 'A woman.' 'A maiden or a married woman?' She answered, 'A maiden.' 'Are you pure or impure?' She answered, 'Pure.' And behold, a woman, the purest of women, was lying at his feet" (Ruth Rabbah 6:1). The rabbis wonder why Boaz was startled by Ruth. In filling in the lacuna in the biblical text, they probe the peculiar word that is used to describe Boaz's response—*vayilafet* ("twisted round").[20] Envisioning Ruth as a climbing plant, they portray her as stealthily approaching Boaz and then wrapping herself around his body. The awestruck Boaz wakes up and grabs her hair in an attempt to fathom whether she is an evil spirit or a woman. The biblical authors only hint that Boaz regards Ruth as an apparition, but the rabbis, who are fond of folktales about spirits and demons, do not hesitate to tease out the ghostly dimension of the episode.[21] Although the midrashic Ruth assures Boaz that she is not a spirit, it is to no avail. Remaining incredulous, Boaz asks her about her marital status and then about her purity. Interestingly, Boaz's questions, at this point, do not derive solely from his anxieties. They disclose Boaz's increasing curiosity about and attraction to the seductive, tantalizing woman who suddenly appeared at midnight on his threshing floor. In inquiring about Ruth's cleanliness (women must undergo a ritual of purification after menstruation before having sexual relations), he seems to be considering having intercourse with her there and then.[22] It is not clear whether his nocturnal grappling with the ivy-like Ruth, however sensual it may be, in fact leads to a sexual act. The ambiguity in the biblical text is daringly displayed, but the final line of the commentary mitigates the erotic overtones and Moabite shades. Ruth, who is now seen (in an abrupt shift) as humbly lying at Boaz's feet, is hailed for being the "purest of women."

In other commentaries, the option of reading the scene as entailing sexual consummation is ruled out more decisively. One such midrash focuses on the exchange between Naomi and Ruth as the latter returns from the threshing floor at dawn. Why does Naomi ask Ruth "who are you?" (Ruth 3:16), the rabbis ponder; after all, she could hardly have failed to recognize her own daughter-in-law. They then spell out what Naomi really meant: "Are you still a maiden [*penuyah*] or a married woman [*eshet 'ish*]?" Ruth answers unwaveringly: penuyah (Ruth

Rabbah 7:4). It may seem strange that Naomi is asking about marriage, but we need to bear in mind that copulation (*bi'ah*), according to rabbinic law, is a mode of marriage, though an unrespectable one.[23] The midrashic Naomi, in other words, is eager to know more about the details of the nocturnal seduction: Did Ruth have sex with Boaz while luring him to become a redeemer? Ruth's response makes clear that her comportment was without blemish: she remained pure and unmarried.

While most rabbis extol Ruth for being a modest convert, some present disturbing suspicions that her conversion has its limits. In a midrashic elaboration of Naomi's instructions to Ruth just before the threshing floor scene, the two are cast yet again in the roles of tutor and new convert. Reading the verse "And you must bathe and anoint yourself" (Ruth 3:3) allegorically, the rabbis present Naomi as instructing Ruth to "cleanse" herself of her "filthy idolatry" and to anoint herself with "good deeds and righteous demeanor" (Ruth Rabbah 5:12). Ruth's conversion, according to this version, needs to be replenished and reaffirmed: one can never be too sure that she has internalized the rules. A more critical commentary calls into question the very possibility that a Moabite is anything but lustful. In probing the details of Ruth's report to Naomi on her return from Boaz's field, Rabbi Hanin the son of Levi calls attention to a discrepancy in the text: whereas Boaz invites Ruth to cling to his maidens (Ruth 2:8), she claims that he encouraged her to cling to his lads (2:21). The discrepancy in the biblical text is probably the result of a scribal error, but for Rabbi Hanin, the most plausible explanation for Ruth's mention of the male reapers lies in her despicable origins.[24] Ruth is, after all, "a Moabitess" (Ruth Rabbah 5:11) and as such is necessarily inclined to choose dubious options.[25]

The heterogeneity of Ruth Rabbah is such that an entirely different approach, one that runs against the grain, is also presented as valuable. Rabbi Zeira comments, "This scroll tells us nothing either of impurity or purity, either of prohibition or permission. Why was it written? To teach us how great is the reward of those who do deeds of kindness [hesed]" (Ruth Rabbah 2:14). Rather than obsessing about questions of purity and impurity, Rabbi Zeira calls for a refreshing shift of attention to the realm of hesed and its rewards. He thus harks back to the key concept of the biblical text—hesed—and demands that it be regarded as pivotal in the rabbinic world as well.

THE MOTHER OF ROYALTY

If the scales usually tip in favor of Ruth in the Midrash, it is in no small part because of her lofty position as King David's foremother.[26] What better proof of her successful conversion than the fact that she is chosen to be the foremother of the founder of the cherished dynasty? She becomes not only a full member of the Israelite community but one who holds a highly important role in its history. Though Ruth and David probably never met (she is his great-grandmother), the rabbis trace a deep affinity between the two, traits that run in the family. In a renowned midrash on the name "Ruth," Rabbi Yohanan regards it as embodying a clue that explains the bond between Ruth and her descendant. "Ruth," he claims, is a derivation of the verb *rava* (saturate) and as such is linked (via a pun) to David's capacity as a psalmist to shower (*leharvot*) God with hymns and prayers to the point of saturation.[27] In this reading, Ruth becomes a muse of sorts, whose overflowing kindness is a source of inspiration for her gifted great-grandson. That David, according to another midrash, would wake up at midnight to play on his harp and lyre (Ruth Rabbah 6:1) makes him all the more indebted to Ruth's heritage. She too, after all, ventures into unknown worlds at midnight.

Not everyone was capable of grasping the beauty of the bond between David and Ruth. There were those who con-

demned him for his Moabite lineage. Rabbi Abba the son of
Kahana recounts that David once addressed God in a complaint: "How long will they rage against me and say, 'Is he not
of a blemished descent? Is he not a descendant of Ruth the
Moabitess?'" In David's witty response to his opponents, he
calls upon them to reflect on other tainted moments in the history of ancient Israel: "You also, are you not descended from
two sisters?. . . And Tamar who married your ancestor Judah—
is it not a blemished lineage?" (Ruth Rabbah 8:1). Taking his
cue from the elders' blessing at the gate in Ruth 4:11, the midrashic David flaunts the similarities between Ruth's tale and the
stories of the founding mothers of Genesis: Rachel, Leah, and
Tamar. Lineages, he insists, cannot be innocent of blemishes.
Ruth's merit is as great as that of her formidable precursors,
whose questionable transactions and seductions did not make
them less vital to the building of the house of Israel. David does
not refer to Ruth's conversion, but in evoking the elders' blessing, he sets into relief a key episode in his great-grandmother's
life, one in which she was fully accepted, before the law, at the
town gate, as part of the Israelite community.

Ruth's spirit hovers not only over David's life but also over
that of his son, King Solomon. On the wings of midrashic
imagination, Ruth is transferred to the most dramatic scene
in Solomon's court. She did not die, we are told, "until she saw
Solomon, the son of her son, sitting and judging the case of the
harlots" (Ruth Rabbah 2:2). In staging this imaginary scene, the
rabbis place Solomon's mother, Bathsheba, on her throne, and
position Ruth, the mother of the dynasty, at an even more elevated spot, by Solomon's right hand.[28] Ruth, apparently, is an
inspirational model not only for David but also for Solomon.
She sits beside him to observe the young king as he confronts a
truly impossible court case. Two prostitutes approach Solomon
asking him to administer justice. Each has recently given birth

to a child, but the child of one died in the night. One of the
mothers accuses the other of switching the dead child for a living one. But the other is just as resolute: "No, for my son is the
living one and your son is dead" (1 Kings 3:22). There are no
witnesses, and nothing in the women's presentation could make
one version more credible than the other. Solomon's response
is utterly unexpected: he orders that the child be cut in half,
thus providing each mother with an equal portion. What seems
initially as a cruel and senseless verdict turns out to be the wis-
est: the true mother hastens to withdraw her claim in order to
spare the child's life.[29] Ruth needs to attend this particular trial
not only to see her descendant in his moment of glory but also
in order to witness a rare moment in which a scorned woman
is revealed as exceptionally virtuous and courageous. Indirectly,
this commentary also serves as one more antidote to those who
regard Ruth as a disrespectful, lewd Moabite woman.

Within the framework of another midrashic line, Ruth becomes more than the mother of historical dynasties. She is
raised to the position of being the foremother of none other
than the Messiah. The beginnings of Jewish messianism lie in
biblical prophecies of salvific events in the end of days. The
prophets dream of a future savior (Isaiah even envisions him as
being of the "root of Jesse"), but it is only in rabbinic culture
that the configuration of the Messiah as the son of David becomes a major trope.[30] That the book of Ruth concludes with
King David seems from the rabbis' perspective to be an indication that the tale anticipates the coming of the Messiah, the
son of David. The marks of the Messiah are revealed at various
points, among them the scene in which Boaz invites Ruth to
join the harvesters' meal (Ruth 2:14). The rabbis envision the
meal as a window to future feasts in the messianic age (Ruth
Rabbah 5:6). In another commentary, the comforting words
of the women neighbors to Naomi in the concluding scene—

"Blessed is the Lord, Who has not deprived you of a redeemer today" (Ruth 4:14)—are construed as referring to the Messiah, the illustrious offspring of the house of David "who shall hold dominion and rule over Israel forever" (Ruth Rabbah 7:15). Although the term "redeemer," *go'el*, in the book of Ruth is primarily a legal one, here it is perceived as referring to the messianic redeemer who will be sent by God to rescue his people and rule over them for all time.[31]

With the growing impact of Christianity, the goal of confronting Christian beliefs gradually became more pressing. There are very few Christian exegetical writings on the book of Ruth in Late Antiquity (this is true of later periods as well), and those that were written were by and large rather marginal.[32] But what did have far more resonance for Christians—from Late Antiquity on—is the evocation of Ruth in the New Testament. In Matthew's opening genealogy, we are told that "Boaz begat Obed of Ruth" (1:5). Unlike the concluding genealogy of the book of Ruth, this lineage culminates not with King David but rather with "Joseph the husband of Mary, of whom was born Jesus, who is called Christ" (Matthew 1:16).[33] Matthew, in other words, turns Ruth into the foremother of Christ, the embodiment of the Christian Messiah. Between the lines, he regards Ruth as a prefiguration of Mary, a notion that will become central in European art, as we shall see. To return to the rabbis, we may surmise that they wanted to have their own version of the story of the birth of the Messiah, the son of David.[34] And it is their own Ruth, the esteemed mother of royalty, who allows them to do so. If the miraculous element in Mary's life is her immaculate conception, Ruth's midrashic life reveals another kind of miracle: that of a lowly Moabite woman whose determination to convert and passionate adherence to God and the Israelite community ultimately make the foundation of the Davidic dynasty and the messianic line possible. In transforming

Ruth into a convert, the Midrash endows her with a new life, precisely because her tale is made compatible with the major concerns of rabbinic Judaism.

The custom of reading the book of Ruth during the Feast of Weeks, Shavuot, first emerged in a late phase of rabbinic Judaism, in the period of the Geonim (between 589 and 1038 CE). There is nothing like ritual to enhance the longevity of characters. That Ruth's tale generates numerous afterlives in the Jewish world—far more than in the Christian context—is in part indebted to its ceremonial role. We have no records of the rabbinic discussion regarding the decision to add the book to the holiday's liturgical corpus, but the fact that Ruth's tale takes place during the harvest season must have made it a compelling supplement to the celebration of a holiday that is defined in the Bible as a harvest feast (Exodus 34:22).

Within the rabbinic world, however, Shavuot is not only an agricultural holiday. It acquires additional significance as a feast that commemorates the giving of the Torah, *matan Torah*, at Mount Sinai. The rabbis deduced that the number of weeks that passed between the Exodus from Egypt and the event at Mount Sinai is equivalent to the number of weeks between Passover and Shavuot. But how is the book of Ruth related to the giving of the Torah at Sinai? We can count on the rabbis to find several innovative connections. Two Talmudists, writing in the eleventh century, offer intriguing links. In *Lekach Tov*, Tobiah ben Eliezer calls attention to the centrality of hesed in both cases: "Why is this scroll read during *Shavuot?* Because this scroll is wholly devoted to hesed and the Torah is all about hesed . . . and was given on Shavuot."[35] Simhah ben Samuel of Vitry explores another trajectory.[36] In *Machzor Vitry*, he draws a comparison between Ruth's tale and the story of the children of Israel at Sinai. Much like her, they undergo a ritual of conversion, as it were, when they accept God's commandments and find shelter under divine wings. If the biblical laws regarding the ger call upon the Israelites to remember their past as gerim, as strangers in a strange land (Deuteronomy 24:18), Simhah ben Samuel of Vitry holds a mirror to his readers and invites them to regard themselves as Ruth and acknowledge the ways in which they too were converts of sorts, seeking a new beginning along an arduous road.

3

◆◄◆►◆

The Shekhinah in Exile

WHEN RUTH STEPS into the tomes of the Zohar, the pin-
nacle of medieval Jewish mysticism, she is endowed with heavenly traits and becomes one of the embodiments of the Shekhinah. But her new divine position does not make her life any
easier. Ruth is envisioned, above all, as a Shekhinah in exile,
forever striving to mend ruptures both in the earthly spheres
and in the upper worlds.

The history of the exilic Shekhinah begins in rabbinic culture. In a well-known Talmudic passage the Shekhinah is associated with times of exile: "In every exile into which the children of Israel went, the Shekhinah was with them."[1] Within the
rabbinic framework this only means that God's presence was
always with Israel in its exiles. But in the Zohar, the Shekhinah
rises to be a character of her own, a full-fledged feminine force
within the Godhead, and as such is fully involved in the agonies
of her people. In fact, she struggles on behalf of the exiled chil-

64

dren of Israel as they wander among the nations of the world and is their heavenly representative. And yet the Zoharic Shekhinah is not only concerned with human affairs; she also plays a major role in internal heavenly dramas. The major rift in the heavenly spheres is between the Shekhinah and her spouse, the blessed Holy One. The two lovers are more often than not separated from each other, or unable to consummate their love, set as they are in a celestial exilic condition. Although these human and divine exiles occur on separate planes, they are inextricably connected. The exile below has ramifications within the heavenly spheres and vice versa. As long as the Shekhinah is in exile above, no redemption in the human world is possible.[2]

The Zoharic Shekhinah is imagined via a network of feminine symbols. She is the Assembly of Israel, the heavenly Jerusalem, a queen, the moon, the earth, the sea, the doe of dawn, and a rose. But she is also associated with several biblical women, among them Ruth.[3] Why Ruth was construed as the Shekhinah's embodiment is a complex question. As we shall see, Ruth's charm for the Kabbalists, the medieval mystics, has much to do with the migratory dimension of her tale. As one who knows only too well what being uprooted entails, Ruth seemed to be most suitable for the role of the exilic Shekhinah.

The question of exile had special urgency as the Zohar was being composed in the late thirteenth century in Castile. As a minority, Jews held a high degree of cultural autonomy and were granted the right to preserve their religious practices, but they were looked down upon as inferior outsiders. What is more, they were under constant pressure to convert to Christianity. King Alfonso X commissioned translations of both the Talmud and the Qur'an into Castilian, in part out of scholarly interest but also as an aid to enhance missionary goals. The book of Ruth had much to offer to this particular Jewish Spanish community. It provided a tale about a cherished woman who chose to convert to Judaism (Ruth continues to be a convert in medieval exegesis), proving the desirability of the Jewish faith, while serving as a rich turf upon which to explore the agonies of living as a stranger in a strange land. The tensions with the Christian world, however, did not preclude a fascination with new trends in medieval Spanish culture. The rise of the Shekhinah in thirteenth-century Spain may be construed as a Jewish response to the growing popularity of the cult of Mary. It is difficult to assess the degree of cross-cultural exchange with any certainty. But the Kabbalists must have been at least partially exposed to the emergence of Mary as a deified mother in the popular culture that surrounded them—be it street processions, sacred dramas enacted on her holy days, or roadside shrines.[4] We can imagine that in rethinking Ruth's role as the foremother of the Messiah, the Kabbalists were eager to upgrade her position and turn her into a deified messianic mother. But they did it their way. They wanted a messianic heavenly mother who would have compassion for an entire community, mourn their dire condition in exile, and intervene on their behalf in the upper world.[5]

Nothing of this Spanish background, however, is mentioned explicitly in the Zohar. The Zohar represents itself as an exegetical compendium that was composed in the circle of Rabbi Shim'on son of Yohai, a famous sage of the second century CE. For many centuries the Zohar was accepted as an authentic commentary of Late Antiquity, but its pseudepigraphic character was laid bare in the twentieth century by the renowned scholar of Kabbalah Gershom Scholem. In one of the foundational studies of Kabbalah, Scholem designated the Spanish Kabbalist Moshe de León (c. 1240–1305) as the true author of the Zohar. Subsequent generations of Kabbalah scholars modified Scholem's findings, regarding the Zohar as the product of the collective creativity of Moshe de León and his fellow exegetes in thirteenth-century Castile.[6]

In concealing their authorship, the Zohar's authors also erase the location where they composed their work. What their writings reveal, however implicitly, is that the rabbinic beit midrash is no longer the privileged site of study. The Zohar portrays the sages as a group of companions walking across the hills of the Galilee while discussing exegetical questions. Relinquishing the restricted space of the traditional house of study, the companions roam the roads like medieval troubadours. It is a distinctly male world; no women accompany them. Yet their wanderings are not devoid of a feminine presence. As they walk and expound upon the Torah, the wandering Shekhinah hovers above them. If she is constantly on their minds, it is also because she is supposedly out there traveling with them in quest of exegetical adventures.

The Zohar is written in midrashic style in Aramaic or Zoharic Aramaic. It exhibits many familiar features of the Midrash: the display of clusters of diverse commentaries by different sages, the attention to minute details in the biblical text, and the search for interconnections between biblical scenes. Where the Zohar clearly departs from midrashic hermeneutics is in its commitment to a mystical interpretive line of inquiry. Biblical verses are seen as embodying distinct secrets, or gates, that lead to the mysteries in the heavenly spheres. The Zohar's authors delve into such enigmas though they never fully clarify their exegetical routes. They are deliberately obscure, and their elucidation at times offers more riddles than answers. But that is precisely one of the pleasures offered by Zoharic commentaries: the invitation to enter an enchanted world where everything is encrypted and one enigma leads to another.

Ruth appears in two major compilations of Zoharic exegesis: *Midrash Ha-Ne'lam* and the main body of the Zohar (*guf ha-Zohar*). The two compilations were composed by Moshe de León and his circle—the main body of the Zohar in the 1280s and *Midrash Ha-Ne'lam* in the preceding decades.[7] Though these compilations were written by the same team, the differences between them attest to changing perceptions and an openness to experiment with new interpretive modes. In *Midrash Ha-Ne'lam*, Ruth's role as Shekhinah is dramatized and has an allegorical bent, whereas in the main body of the Zohar she stands for the Shekhinah in a more subtle and encoded way. In both cases, however, the fact that Ruth is a Shekhinah does not stop her from appearing on occasion in human form. The Kabbalists are fond of paradoxes and contradictions, even more than were the rabbis of Late Antiquity. That Ruth can glide freely from heaven to earth and then ascend back to the heavenly spheres only makes her, in mystical eyes, all the more wondrous.

Midrash Ha-Ne'lam contains a section with an extensive exposition of the book of Ruth.[8] In this near verse-by-verse commentary, the authors adopt the midrashic configuration of Ruth as a convert, though they take the rabbinic praise a step further. Ruth's conversion, they argue, did not take place on the road but happened earlier, in Moab. Ruth converted before marrying Mahlon, and in the course of her conversion she changed her name. Initially, Ruth was called Gilit (they speculate), but on becoming Mahlon's wife she received a Hebrew name: Ruth (this is probably the first reference to "Ruth" as a name of a woman convert).[9] In another Zoharic commentary, Rabbi Yose passionately proclaims, "I would be astonished if this scroll came only to trace the lineage of David back to Ruth the Moabite, and nothing more!" He suggests that the scroll's great merit does not stem from Ruth's association with the Davidic dynasty, but rather from its depiction of a "righteous woman [who] came to convert and to be enveloped beneath the wings of *Shekhinah*—teaching about her humility and modesty."[10]

But the Zoharic authors' free spirit of exploration becomes even more pronounced and intriguing when they depart more radically from rabbinic tradition and envision Ruth not only as a human convert "enveloped beneath the wings of *Shekhinah*" but as the Shekhinah herself, or rather as the exilic Shekhinah. They move away from the world of the rabbis both in deifying Ruth and in their attention to her migratory experiences. Instead of domesticating Ruth—instead of placing her within the domain of a house with a mezuzah—they highlight her sense of dislocation as well as some of the painful features of her life.

In searching for the traces of the exilic Shekhinah, the Kabbalists were primarily drawn to the threshing floor scene. It is no surprise that the nocturnal encounter of Ruth and Boaz, with its distinctly enigmatic character, compelled them. They sought, however, to mold the mysteries of this harvest night as mystical, and so they project the scene onto the upper worlds. The threshing floor in *Midrash Ha-Ne'lam* is not quite an earthly one. It is set in heaven, where Ruth appears as the Shekhinah and Boaz represents the blessed Holy One.[11] When the supernal Boaz lies down at the foot of the heap of grain on the threshing floor, he first delights in "consuming heavenly life" and looks forward to his sexual union with his divine consort. But life in heaven has its own ruptures. At midnight, Boaz is startled by the sight of the grief-stricken Shekhinah lying by his feet:

> And it happened at midnight that the man trembled and twisted round [Ruth 3:8].[12] Why? Because *Behold! There was a woman lying at his feet!*—lying in the dust crushed by His feet—this is Assembly of Israel. Then, at that moment, she was aroused toward him and he asked her, saying "My daughter, *who are you?* [Ruth 3:9] in exile? Who are you at this moment?" And she replied, "*I am Ruth, your handmaid*—brimming with sorrow, overflowing with pain over my children in exile, and over the holy palaces, for I have been exiled from My sanctuary. And it is not enough that I have been banished, but they abuse and curse Me every day on account of them, and I have no voice in exile to respond."[13]

We are never told explicitly that Ruth is the Shekhinah, but we are called upon to see her as such given that she is designated as the Assembly of Israel and speaks on behalf of her people. In many ways, this allegorical commentary is as far as one can get from the book of Ruth, and yet it is attuned to the darker shades of the biblical account of the threshing floor scene. Ruth, after all, would not have sneaked on to the threshing floor at night if she were not a desperate migrant gleaner struggling to survive.[14] The terse biblical text provides no window to Ruth's feelings at this point, leaving the Zohar's authors plenty of room to improvise. They do so by underscoring the humiliating dimension of Ruth's lying at Boaz's feet. The Zoharic Ruth does not just lie at his feet, but rather wallows in the dust, utterly "crushed." To Boaz's question "Who are you at this moment?" she responds with a poignant depiction of herself: "brimming with sorrow, overflowing with pain" due to the dire state of her exiled children and the destruction of the Temple.[15] Though the fallen Shekhinah bemoans her lost voice in exile, she forcefully voices her complaint. She bears a resemblance to the exiles who cry by the rivers of Babylon, regarding the singing of psalms on foreign soil as impossible, while, paradoxically, insisting on delivering their mournful song (see Psalms 137).

What makes the nocturnal exchange between Ruth and Boaz all the more appealing from a Zoharic perspective is the recurrent use of the term "redeemer," *go'el*. The biblical Ruth primarily uses *go'el* as a legal term, but the Zohar sees her quest for a redeemer as a quest for a messianic salvation that would end the miseries of exile. They follow the rabbis in associating Ruth with salvific matters, but opt for a different track. No longer merely a foremother of the Messiah, the son of David, Ruth here becomes an agent of redemption herself, a heavenly messianic mother who calls attention to the plight of her exiled children and tries to shake heaven and earth on their behalf. Haviva Pedaya ventures to propose that the Shekhinah was "born," as it were, on the day of the destruction of the Temple.[16] This catastrophic event and the subsequent exile do not mark the end of the drama but rather a moment of birth, in which the Shekhinah springs to life and acquires a major role in conveying the great need for salvation. Although the Shekhinah is the lowest emanation in the Godhead, and as such depends on her male consort, she looms large as the primary mediator between the divine and human worlds in times of exile.

In responding to Ruth's cry, the blessed Holy One utters Boaz's words with a few mystical supplements: "*Stay for the night* (Ruth 3:13)—stay now in exile and guide Your children there with Torah and good deeds. If their good deeds aid Your redemption, You will be redeemed. If not, [then in the morning . . .] *I will redeem you myself* [Ruth 3:13]. . . . For morning and the light of redemption will come."[17] The supernal Boaz is willing to act as redeemer, but not immediately. The morning and light of redemption are destined to come, he promises, but in the meantime the night of exile prevails, and Ruth must stay and wait. This nocturnal exchange on the threshing floor serves as a sobering reminder that messianic aspirations are all too often deferred in reality. The deferral of the coming of the Messiah is, in fact, a pivotal concern in Jewish exegesis.[18] The coming of the Messiah seems both imminent and distant, and accordingly the much sought-after redemption is forever suspended. This notion originated in rabbinic literature, but it becomes more salient in medieval Jewish mysticism and beyond. Indeed, the peculiar absurdity of messianic yearning even caught Franz Kafka's attention. Probing the paradoxical character of the Messiah, Kafka adds a modernist touch: "The Messiah will come only when he is no longer necessary; he will come only on the day after his arrival; he will come, not on the last day, but on the very last."[19]

In *Midrash Ha-Ne'lam*, Ruth is singled out for her capacity to "stay for the night" and refrain from action while awaiting redemption. In the sequence that follows, Ruth's inaction is presented as being as admirable as that of the fugitive David. In one of the most moving episodes in the book of Samuel, David flees Jerusalem with his men after Absalom usurps his throne. On their way, Shimei son of Gera from the clan of Saul hurls stones at them and curses David with spiteful vengeance: "Get out, get out, you man of blood, you worthless fellow! The Lord has brought back upon you all the blood of the house of Saul, in whose place you became king, and the Lord has given the kingship into the hand of Absalom your son, and here you are, because of your evil, for you are a man of blood" (2 Samuel 16:7–8). Mercilessly, Shimei settles a score with David for assuming power at the expense of the house of Saul. But David remains silent. When one of the warriors questions his lack of response, David replies, "If he curses, it is because the Lord has said to him, 'Curse David,' and who can say, 'Why have you done this?'" He then turns to his men and elaborates: "Look— my son, the issue of my loins, seeks my life. How much more so, then, this Benjaminite. Leave him be and let him curse. . . . Perhaps the Lord will see my affliction and the Lord may requite me good for his cursing this day" (16:10–12). The proud and often implacable David is unexpectedly willing, at this low point of his life, to accept a humiliating blow from a man he could have killed. David's inaction discloses his acute pain on witnessing the rebellion of his own son against him. Another stab in the heart from a mere Benjaminite could hardly matter. And yet while the melancholy dethroned king unleashes his agony and acknowledges the impossibility of fathoming divine motives, he remains stubbornly hopeful that God may ultimately enable him to prevail. The power of David's inaction did not escape the Zohar's authors, who hail his restraint: "Shimei came out from among the Benjaminites toward the anointed one, blaspheming and cursing him—but he was silent. Never had there been blasphemy like that, but he felt no need to respond, remaining silent."[20] Drawing a comparison between Ruth on the threshing floor and the episode of David and Shimei requires a leap of the imagination.[21] It is not a noticeable connection in the biblical text. But by juxtaposing the migrant Ruth and the fugitive David, the Zohar highlights an intriguing similarity between the stories of these two biblical characters: their acute agonies, exceptional perseverance, and capacity for unpredictable moves.

In explicating Ruth's merit, the Zohar's authors combine their commentary on "stay for the night" with a consideration of Boaz's expression of gratitude for Ruth's hesed (Ruth 3:10). If the biblical Boaz praises Ruth for clinging to him rather than to younger men, the supernal Boaz is touched by the kindness and faithfulness of the exilic Shekhinah toward him: "Even now in exile you have treated me with abundant goodness and faithfulness. . . . And you did not doubt even after the scorn and blasphemy of the other nations."[22] The blessed Holy One assures Ruth that even if her children fail to mend their ways, he will nonetheless bring salvation at the end of the night. The resilient and loyal biblical gleaner becomes in *Midrash Ha-Ne'lam* a cherished model for all those who aspire to preserve hope for a redeeming future, even during the long, humiliating night of exile.

REVISITING SODOM: A HERETICAL PERSPECTIVE

We encounter another mystical Ruth in the later corpus of the main body of the Zohar. Here the commentaries on the book of Ruth are few but have a distinct verve. Within this exegetical framework, Ruth's position as Shekhinah remains encrypted and is nowhere dramatized, whereas her role as a woman receives much attention. But even when Ruth appears in human form, she is not quite an ordinary woman. Intervening in heavenly matters is among her most noteworthy activities.

The threshing floor scene is a privileged scene in the main body of the Zohar as well. In this version, however, Ruth's glory is displayed not in patient waiting but in bold action. In addition to preserving the familial line against all odds, she ventures to intervene in the heavenly world and pave the way to redemption. The messianic era and the end of exile may be continuously deferred, but human agency matters. Ruth, in fact, is among the select mortals who can play an active role in ushering the advent of the Messiah.

Acquiring a heretical spirit in the course of time, the Zohar's authors, at this point of their work together, are also drawn to the darker, ambiguous aspects of the nocturnal encounter. They go so far as to present the scene at the cave by Sodom as a prerequisite for Ruth's allurement of Boaz and ultimately for the birth of the Messiah. It may come as a shock to modern readers that the Zohar finds a redemptive potential in Sodom, but this is precisely the point: to search for salvation where it is least expected. In a renowned essay titled "Redemption Through Sin," Gershom Scholem marvels at the paradox embedded in the mystical perception of redemption, most evident in the assumption that transgressive deeds may lead to a messianic era.[23] According to the Talmud, a divine commandment (a mitzvah) that "comes through transgression" is a legal concept relevant to cases such as building a *sukkah* from stolen materials. In the Kabbalists' revisionary take on it, a mitzvah may come through sin because transgressions—especially ritual or sexual transgressions—can potentially further the fulfillment of the divine plan. Scholem focuses on the false messiahs of the seventeenth and eighteenth centuries, Shabbtai Zevi and Jacob Frank, but his observations are also pertinent to earlier periods of Jewish mysticism.[24] In the main body of the Zohar, we can already detect a fascination with the blend of sin, sexuality, and sacredness in reflections on the coming of the Messiah.[25] Because this blend is unimaginable, it seems to convey most succinctly the wondrous character of redemption, always emerging from unpredictable directions.

Rabbi Yitzhak's commentary on the hidden aspects of the

notorious inception of Moab and Ammon at the cave by Sodom sheds light on this heretical logic: "Come and see: From Lot and his daughters issued two separate nations, linked to the side befitting them. So the blessed Holy One revolves revolutions, rotates rotations in the world, so that all will turn out fittingly, all linked to its site. . . . It would have been more seemly for Lot had the blessed Holy One engendered these two nations from him and his wife, but it was in order for them to be linked to the site befitting them."[26] Rabbi Yitzhak admits that it would have been more "seemly" if Lot and his wife had been the parents of Moab and Ammon. But it is not a coincidence that the two founding fathers of these nations are the outcome of the incestuous union between Lot and his daughters. The transgressive deeds of the two daughters, he claims, ensure the linking of Ammon and Moab to the realm that most befits them: the side of the demonic, the *sitra ahra*. What thrills Rabbi Yitzhak is not so much the punitive aspect of this relegation of Israel's enemies to the demonic realm, but rather its unforeseen consequences. While revolving celestial wheels, "revolving revolutions," God can, unpredictably, turn sinful moments into redemptive ones. Thus Sodom's cave can serve as a springboard to Bethlehem's threshing floor. Those who suppose that familiar phenomena will endure in their original form fail to understand the marvels of divine conduct. As a grand salvific potter, the blessed Holy One never hesitates to transform one vessel into another.

The redeeming dimension of the cave scene is laid bare more explicitly in Rabbi Yose's ensuing commentary. Building upon the most minute textual links between the two biblical tales (specifically, Genesis 19:33 and Ruth 3:14), Rabbi Yose points out that Ruth on the threshing floor, much like Lot's daughters in the cave, lies down and then rises without being noticed. He singles out in particular the affinity between Ruth and Lot's elder daughter, the foremother of Moab.[27] Lot's elder daughter is far more distinguished than her sister because in the depiction of her rise after lying with Lot the word *kuma* (rise) is spelled with the letter *vav*, which occurs in the divine name (in the biblical account of the sister's rise, the word is spelled without a *vav*). Every scriptural letter counts—all the more so when it is associated with a divine name. Marked by a divine touch, Lot's elder daughter deserves to participate in a supernal act from which "King Messiah was destined to issue."[28] As Ruth Kara-Ivanov Kaniel points out, both the Zoharic Ruth and her Moabite foremother are construed as vital to the rise of the house of David and the advancement of a messianic era.[29] The transgressive bent of their deeds is not condemned but rather seen as an acknowledgment that mystical transformative acts necessarily appear in highly diverse forms. Seductive foreign women may turn out to be salvific. The wonder embedded in the positioning of Ruth the Moabite at the very foundation of the Davidic dynasty in the biblical text itself is thus set forth in bold, heretical strokes.

JOINING FORCES WITH TAMAR: REPAIRING THE WORLD

In reimagining the threshing floor scene, the main body of the Zohar also flaunts Ruth's affinity with another foreign seducer: Tamar. Tamar, however, is less transgressive than Lot's elder daughter, a distinction that makes her a full-fledged partner of Ruth.[30] Over the chasm of time, the two widows join forces to rescue the line of Judah.

> There were two women through whom the seed of Judah was established, from whom issued King David, King Solomon, and King Messiah. These two women correspond to one another: Tamar and Ruth, whose husbands died first, who exerted themselves in this action. Tamar enticed [*hishtadlah*] her father-in-law, who was next of kin to his sons who had died. Why did she entice him? As is written: *for she saw that Shelah had grown up and she had not been given to him as*

wife. . . . As for Ruth, her husband died and then she engaged [*hishtadlah*] in this act with Boaz, as is written: *She uncovered his feet and lay down* (Ruth 3:7). Engaging with him, she later gave birth to Obed. Now you might ask "Why didn't Obed issue from another woman?" But precisely she was needed, no one else. From these two, the seed of Judah was established and consummated. Both of them acted properly, acting kindly toward the dead so that the world would later be enhanced [*letaken olam*]. This corresponds to what is said: *I praise the dead, who have already died* (Ecclesiastes 4:2), because when they were first alive, they were not praiseworthy, but later they were. Both of them exerted themselves to act kindly [*hesed*] and faithfully toward the dead, and the blessed Holy One assisted in that act. All was fitting! Happy is the one who engages [*she-mishtadel*] in Torah day and night.[31]

In luring the reluctant Judah and Boaz to implement the levirate law and become redeemers, Tamar and Ruth, we are told, acted "properly." A disruption in familial continuity, the lack of offspring, is a grand disaster that brings havoc to both the world below and the world above. It is only thanks to the courageous determination of Tamar and Ruth to repair the world (*letaken olam*) that the lineage of Judah survived and the flow of life could resume its course, leading to the births of "King David, King Solomon, and King Messiah." The repair of the world goes beyond the earthly spheres and has a ripple effect in the heavenly spheres as well. The blessed Holy One is drawn into the drama and assists the two widows in their act of hesed. A blissful correspondence between the human and divine worlds may thus evolve, or in Zoharic terms: "All was fitting!"

As always, the Zohar's authors juggle biblical verses in substantiating their claims. They justify Tamar's seduction of Judah by citing the verse that indicates that the latter had not kept his promise: "for she saw that Shelah had grown up and she had not been given to him as wife" (Genesis 38:14). Their exegetical flair, however, is far more striking in their treatment of Ruth's tale. Of the different details of the threshing floor scene, they dwell on the most provocative and obscure: "She uncovered his feet and lay down" (Ruth 3:7). Without fully explicating their reasoning, they intimate that instead of searching for the messianic dimension of this night only in the explicit use of the terms *redeem* and *redeemer* in the exchange between Ruth and Boaz, we need to consider the more ambiguous, erotic act of uncovering the feet. They go on to insist that the uncovering on the threshing floor was not merely flirtatious but outright sexual. Much like Tamar, Ruth became pregnant immediately. It was on the very night of Ruth's "engaging" with Boaz on the threshing floor that Obed was conceived. To those who might doubt Ruth's merit or position as the great foremother of the Davidic messianic line, the Zohar makes clear that it is precisely Ruth who was needed for the task; she was the only one who could rescue her dead husband, Mahlon, from oblivion and ensure the continuity between past and future generations.[32]

To the mélange of verses from Genesis and the book of Ruth, the Zohar's authors add a line from Ecclesiastes: "I praise the dead, who have already died" (4:2). In Ecclesiastes the verse is a bitterly ironic statement whose purpose is to present death as preferable to life. In this Zoharic passage, however, it is whimsically taken to be literal. The dead husbands of Tamar and Ruth, who did little of note when they were alive, became "praiseworthy" only on dying. After all it is their death that led to the admirable initiatives of their wives.

In a strange twist at the end of this commentary, the efforts of Tamar and Ruth to repair the familial line and the world are presented as analogous to the exultant studying of Torah day and night. The same Aramaic verb, *ishtaddalat* (related to the Hebrew *hishtadlut*)—which spans a wide spectrum of meaning: engage, devote oneself, exert oneself, strive, wrestle, entice—is used both in the depiction of the seductive acts of the two women and in the account of Torah study.[33] This perplexing analogy makes perfect sense in the Zoharic world, where the study of Torah is a highly erotic activity. Every night (with the exception of the Sabbath eve), the companions arise in order to study the Torah.[34] It is another unconventional mode of study (the nocturnal counterpart to the wanderings on the road), for they begin at midnight, when most humans are sound asleep, and continue till dawn.[35] Melila Hellner-Eshed explicates the erotic-mystical quality of this nocturnal ritual: "The nocturnal study of the mystics below beautifies and adorns the Shekhinah, making her desirable to her lover, the blessed Holy One. In the soft, dim light of dawn . . . [t]he two then enjoy complete union— *zivvug* (coupling)—full of love and eros, drawing down blessings into all reality."[36] The Zohar's quest for marital harmony in heaven is a quest for a state of redemption in which there shall be perfection above and below, and all worlds shall be united in one bond. The Kabbalists, however, do not merely hope for redress. They are mystical activists, as it were, whose objective is theurgic: to repair the fissures between the exilic Shekhinah and the blessed Holy One, as well as between the Shekhinah and the human sphere.

Although both women are associated with the companions' engagement with Torah, Ruth's tale is more pertinent. Midnight is the climactic moment of her seduction of Boaz on the threshing floor. What is more, Ruth's descendant, David, is the primary model for the Kabbalists' nocturnal delights. The companions perceive themselves as emulating the midrashic David, who would wake up at midnight to play his harp and lyre and to shower God with his psalms. But given that Ruth is also associated with her descendant's blissful saturation, she turns out to be a hidden source of inspiration for David's medieval, mystical followers as well.[37]

And yet even the more uplifting renditions of Ruth in the main body of the Zohar are set in an exilic world. Ruth's engagement, ishtaddalat, much like the nocturnal ritual of the companions, leaves a stamp on both the lower and upper worlds, but exile never really comes to an end. Messianic times may be closer, may seem more tangible, but they remain beyond reach. The only prerogative that is left is to relentlessly seek the repair of the world.

THE KABBALISTS' SHAVUOT: RUTH AS TORAH

What is the Kabbalists' view of Ruth's relevance to Shavuot, the Feast of Weeks? The Zohar's authors, much like their rabbinic precursors, sought meaningful links between the book of Ruth and the giving of the Torah on Shavuot. But rather than looking for similar traits between Ruth and the Torah, they turned Ruth herself into the Torah. In *Midrash Ha-Ne'lam*, the fact (or the Zoharic fact) that the Torah is one of the many facets of the Shekhinah is seen as a clear-cut indication that Ruth too, as the embodiment of the Shekhinah, stands for Holy Writ. Reading her "scroll" on Shavuot is thus most suitable for a holiday that is devoted to the celebration of the Torah.[38] Another commentary in this compilation finds additional clues for the association of Ruth with the Torah encrypted in her name. How? It is a rather circuitous and wild exegetical road. The Zoharic contemplation begins with the rabbinic midrash that sees Ruth's name as a derivation of the verb "to saturate." In this version, however, it is Ruth (rather than David) who "saturates the blessed Holy One with songs and praises perpetually."[39] Once Ruth becomes a singer she can be linked to the turtledove, the *tor*, of the Song of Songs whose exquisite voice is heard in the land in springtime (2:12). Ruth's name corroborates the connection: *rut* and *tor* consist of the same letters—*resh, vav, taf*—though in reverse order. The next step in this playful juggling requires a leap from *tor* to *torah*. This leap relies not solely on the phonetic similarity between the two terms but also on the allegorical readings of the Song of Songs. In

Song of Songs Rabbah, the Song's language of love is regarded as a key to understanding the great bond that is formed between God and Israel in Exodus, beginning with the departure from Egypt and culminating at Sinai.[40] The turtledove's role within this exegetical framework is to serve as the harbinger of redemption and divine love. The link between *tor* and *torah* thus becomes inevitable from a Zoharic perspective. This particular tor is inextricably connected to the foundational events of Israel and to the sealing of the amorous covenant between God and his people at Sinai. There is some logic in this bewildering sequence: if Ruth is tor and tor is Torah, then Ruth is Torah!

In a later Zoharic text, *Tikkunei Zohar*, composed in the early fourteenth century (presumably after Moshe de León's death), the question of the link between Ruth's name and the Torah is raised once again. *Tikkunei Zohar* primarily elaborates on the accounts of *Midrash Ha-Ne'lam* regarding the fallen, exilic Shekhinah on the threshing floor, but it also develops the commentary on the ties between *rut, torah,* and *tor.*[41] In this case, the affinities among the three words are deciphered through the distribution of the letters of the divine name among the different characters of the book of Ruth. It so happens that the letter *he* "clings" to Ruth's name, and thus enables the transformation of *rut* to *torah* (*taf, vav, resh, he*). The turtledove, the tor, serves as a mediator and its importance is acknowledged: "It is said of Ruth: the voice of the turtledove is heard in our land."[42]

In both of these Zoharic texts, the giving of the Torah is a blissful pause in the long night of exile, an exhilarating event in which the Ruth-like Shekhinah can rise from the dust and bask in the light of love. Earlier we noted that the Shekhinah was "born" on the day on which the Temple was destroyed, but we could equally say that she was "born" on the day on which Torah was given at Sinai. These two "births" mark two pivotal moments in her life. If the destruction of the Temple turns the

Shekhinah into an agent of redemption, forever struggling on behalf of her exiled children, Mount Sinai turns her into the agent of the grand book—the book whose precious tomes can serve as an antidote to the afflictions that too often threaten to engulf the world. Full of contradictions, Ruth can "brim" with both sorrows and joy as she saturates the upper and lower spheres with her Torah, with the singing of scriptural songs and praises.

While introducing new interpretive perspectives on Shavuot, the Zohar's authors also left a mark on the holiday's rituals. Some two hundred years after the appearance of the Zohar, sixteenth-century Kabbalists invented a new ritual—Tikkun Leil Shavuot. Tikkun Leil Shavuot is a night vigil that is modeled on the Zohar's descriptions of the companions' ritualistic nocturnal Torah study. Above all, it is shaped in light of the Zoharic account of the vigil of vigils held by Rabbi Shim'on and his fellow exegetes on the night of Shavuot. According to this cherished tale, Rabbi Shim'on and his companions convene during the night of Shavuot to prepare for the great festivity of the following day. In their eyes, the giving of the Torah is inseparable from the wedding ceremony of the Shekhinah and her divine consort, which is why they feel the urge to provide the bride with the most refined adornments, *tikkunim* (the term *tikkun* in this context means adornment). What better decoration could they bestow upon the Shekhinah than a necklace of scriptural texts? They sit all night and link diverse verses—beads of sorts—from the three divisions of the Bible: Torah, Prophets, and Writings. Thanks to their efforts, the Shekhinah is perfectly adorned on her glorious wedding day, and the companions have the privilege of rejoicing with her, while "singing the song of Torah."[43] The exilic rift in heaven vanishes momentarily as the Torah is given and the divine lovers unite.

Tikkun Leil Shavuot was apparently first practiced by Joseph Karo (1488–1575) and his followers in Nicopolis in present-day Bulgaria, but it acquired its canonical position only on reaching Safed, in the Galilee, where a group of mystics under the leadership of Rabbi Yitzhak Luria (1534–1572) adopted it as part of their celebration of Shavuot.[44] Taking their cue from Rabbi Shim'on and his companions, the Kabbalists of Safed stayed awake all night and prepared exegetical ornaments. Their list of "beads" is rather variegated: they first recited a chain of verses from diverse biblical texts and then read the 613 mitzvot, and an array of passages from the Mishnah, the Book of Creation, and the Zohar.

The Zohar's commentaries on the book of Ruth are not included in Tikkun Leil Shavuot.[45] Perhaps it was deemed unnecessary to add them, given that the book of Ruth itself is read ceremoniously on the following day of the feast, and as far as the Kabbalists were concerned Ruth's primary life included all her later afterlives. Whatever the reason, the Zoharic Ruth surely hovers in the background of Tikkun Leil Shavuot. She hovers there as one whose deeds are analogous to those of the companions who engage in Torah study at night; she hovers there as an amorous tor, but, above all, she hovers there as one whose tale, with its migratory agonies and redeeming moments, serves as a vital building block of the multi-faceted figure of the Shekhinah.

4

The Pastoral Gleaner

THE IMAGE OF RUTH gleaning peacefully in pastoral land-scapes with sheaves in her hands or by her side is so deeply en-graved in our collective memory that we assume that she was always portrayed this way. And yet Ruth first emerges as a pas-toral gleaner only on the canvas of Nicolas Poussin's magnifi-cent painting *Summer* (1660–1664), with its exquisite blend of biblical themes and classical motifs. Ever since the seventeenth century, pastoral Ruths have appeared in many visual renditions of the book of Ruth and are among the ancient gleaner's most renowned afterlives.

The pastoral mode has a long and intricate history.[1] Its beginnings lie in the work of Theocritus, a Greek poet of the third century BCE. Theocritus's pastoral poems, his *Idylls*, re-volve around the charms of rustic living and abound with de-tailed descriptions of picturesque scenes of rural beauty and innocent tranquillity. Their protagonists are shepherds and goatherds, who pass their time wooing nymphs and holding singing or piping contests. The high point of this pastoral world is midday, a time of leisure, *otium*, when the shepherds rest and devote themselves to poetry and music. Though pastures are the primary backdrop of Theocritus's *Idylls*, other aspects of rural life are also pertinent. One of the pivotal scenes, depicted in idyll 7, takes place during a harvest feast and its celebration of the "good gifts" bestowed by Demeter, the goddess of grain, "with no grudging hand."[2]

Virgil, the leading Roman poet of the first century BCE, embraces Theocritus's pastoral heritage in his *Eclogues* (or *Bucolics*) while introducing several changes. In Virgil's hands, the rural setting of pastoral poetry becomes more distinctly legendary, a place longed for rather than an actual site. If Theocritus's shepherds live in Sicily's countryside, Virgil's protagonists roam about in a paradisiacal Arcadia. The physical Arcadia is a region in the Peloponnese, but in Virgil's *Eclogues* it becomes the privileged location of a Golden Age, where shepherds and rustics live in peace, in harmony with nature. Though blissful harmony prevails in Virgil's pastoral world, it is not uncomplicatedly ideal. Arcadia is not meant to serve as an escape from reality. It is set against the backdrop of wars and confiscations of farmers' lands as an invitation to imagine a better world in which human benevolence is the norm and poetry reigns.[3] What further complicates this bucolic Eden is the shadow of death. At times, dirges replace the joyful singing and tombs of deceased loved ones appear amid the lush, verdant landscapes.

The pastoral almost disappeared during the Middle Ages— it was too pagan for medieval Christian theologians—but it was revived in Renaissance literature and art.[4] Theocritus's *Idylls*, and even more so Virgil's *Eclogues*, exerted a powerful influence on many poets and artists of the Renaissance—from Petrarch, Boccaccio, and Jacopo Sannazaro to Luca Signorelli and Titian. While the Renaissance advocates of the pastoral never hesitated to celebrate its pagan features and offered alluring portrayals of Pan, the god of shepherds and nymphs, they also used this rediscovered mode as a means to reinterpret scriptural texts. The lives of scriptural shepherds—from Jacob and David to Christ—were now construed as analogous to those of shepherds in ancient Greece and Rome.

Ruth was not associated with the pastoral during the Renaissance, but in the work of the heirs of the Renaissance spirit she gradually acquired a central position as a quintessential pastoral figure. The most abundant exegetical scene of the pastoral Ruth is to be found in the world of art—initially in the baroque art of the seventeenth century and later in various schools of modern art. This chapter is devoted to the trendsetters, the French artists who introduced the primary shifts in the visualization of the pastoral Ruth. But the afterlives of the pastoral Ruth are by no means limited to the French context. The pastoral gleaner appears in diverse garbs across Europe and eventually beyond Europe. She even leads a prosperous life on the canvases of early Zionist artists in the twentieth century, a topic we shall explore in detail in the next chapter.

The urge to visualize Ruth, however, did not begin with baroque art. Until the sixteenth and seventeenth centuries, the history of Western art was largely identical with that of ecclesiastical and religious art. Images of Ruth appear in Christian iconography: first in Byzantine art—primarily in illuminated Octateuchs (illustrated reproductions of the first eight books of the Bible)—and later, more extensively, in medieval illuminated Bibles and *Bibles moralisées* (pictorial Bibles that included selected passages from the Bible accompanied by illustrations and commentaries).[5] In the Middle Ages, the Catholic Church made use of pictures as a means of instruction, to supplement the knowledge acquired by oral teaching. Few people outside the ranks of the clergy and the monks could read, which is why frescoes and stained-glass windows depicting biblical scenes were set in many churches. Illuminated manuscripts did not have the same kind of visibility as the frescoes and stained-glass windows, but they were regarded as prized possessions and were often displayed on high holy days. Most of the ecclesiastical artists were unnamed, and their art was meant to represent the church's stance, rather than an individual perspective. How is Ruth perceived in this context? Generally speaking, she is imagined as a highly pious woman. She often appears in fields of wheat or barley, but these rural settings have none of the features of the classical pastoral. Another unusual aspect of Ruth's ecclesiastical renditions is the minimizing of her foreignness. She usually seems to be a local and is dressed as one. We noted earlier that the book of Ruth did not play a major role in Christian exegesis. But in the writings of the few church fathers who did comment on it, the rabbinic concept of Ruth as an exemplary convert was adopted, albeit with some modifications. She was perceived as a pagan who converted to the Christian faith, an interpretive claim corroborated by her position as Christ's ancestor in Matthew's genealogy.[6] Christian iconographers, in turn, endorsed this naturalization of the ancient gleaner and translated it into visual terms.

Ruth has a place of honor in Christian iconography, but she remains a rather marginal figure in this realm. It is only once her tale is seen as the perfect scriptural embodiment of the classical pastoral, only once she steps into the world of the baroque, that she becomes one of the most cherished biblical women of Western art. The pastoral Ruth marks a decisive break with preceding ecclesiastical traditions, but she is also indebted to them. The artists who envision Ruth as a pastoral gleaner, like their anonymous precursors, tend to present her as a local and relegate her foreign attributes to the margins, or even efface them altogether. The choice to downplay Ruth's foreign origin, however, is not solely due to medieval Christian iconography. For painters of the pastoral Ruth there was another good reason for allowing Ruth to blend in with those who surround her. In the Greek and Roman pastoral, there are no foreigners: pastoral scenes revolve around the intricacies of local lives in rural settings.

NICOLAS POUSSIN'S *SUMMER:* THE INAUGURAL LANDSCAPE

The French painter Nicolas Poussin (1594–1665) is the primary inventor of the pastoral Ruth. Poussin was the leading painter of the French baroque style, although he spent most of his life in Rome. He returned to Paris for a brief period to serve as First Painter under Louis XIII and Cardinal Richelieu but then relinquished his position and headed back to Rome. Poussin's determination to live in Rome is inextricably connected to his aesthetic choices and fascination with the great masters of Italian Renaissance art. Fittingly, he was hailed by one critic in 1650 as "the Raphael of our century."[7] In his later years, he devoted more attention to landscapes and had a considerable impact on the development of the genre. If the predominant tendency before the seventeenth century was to regard landscape as background or stage decor, in Poussin's hands it was transformed into an essential element of the composition, the factor that brings together the story and the action. His landscapes are vast, opulent, and teeming with life and power, whether the subject is biblical, mythological, historical, or a blend of all three.[8]

Poussin's painting of Ruth's encounter with Boaz in the field, titled *Summer: Ruth and Boaz,* is among his most renowned landscapes. It is part of a series he worked on in his final years, *The Four Seasons* (*Les Quatre Saisons,* 1660–1664). He was ill at the time, and his hand was shaky, but this physical impediment did not stop him from fashioning one of his grandest masterpieces. The series was commissioned by the duc de Richelieu, the great-nephew of the cardinal, and eventually the four paintings found their way to the Louvre, where they still reside today.

Nicolas Poussin, *Summer: Ruth and Boaz* (1660–1664). Photo copyright
© Musée du Louvre, Dist. RMN-Grand Palais / Angèle Dequier.

In this series, Poussin matches the seasons with successive times
of the day: early morning for spring, midday for summer, evening for autumn, and a moonlit night for winter. "Seeing nature
through the glass of time," as the eighteenth-century essayist
William Hazlitt put it, Poussin introduces into the natural cycle
of the days and seasons selected episodes from human history,
or, rather, from biblical history.[9] For spring he chooses Adam
and Eve in the Garden of Eden; for summer the encounter of
Ruth and Boaz in the field; for autumn, the Israelite spies returning with a cluster of grapes from the Promised Land; and
for winter the story of the Flood. The originality of Poussin's
interpretive choices is striking. No one before Poussin had ever

made connections between the seasons and these particular biblical tales. No one before Poussin had ever portrayed Ruth as emerging from a pastoral landscape of summer.

Let us follow the details of Poussin's interpretive trajectory in *Summer*. The scene is built up in rectangular blocks behind the principal figures in the foreground. Ruth kneels before Boaz (as she is depicted doing in Ruth 2:10), with a bundle of sheaves at her side. She is responding to Boaz's welcoming gesture and his invitation to be a privileged gleaner in his field. Every after-life of Ruth highlights a different episode in her tale. If the Midrash valorizes the oath on the road, and the Zohar endorses the night on the threshing floor as the climactic moment of redemption, in pastoral adaptations of the book of Ruth the encounter between Ruth and Boaz in the field is the favored scene. It has many of the vital ingredients of the pastoral: a peaceful harvest scene in fecund fields, where human goodness prevails. It is here that Boaz's generosity is first displayed, and it is here that a touch of romance is introduced into the tale.

In transferring this scene onto his canvas, Poussin places the vast field of wheat at the center of the painting (he was inspired by the fields of the Roman Campagna). Noontime, the quintessential pastoral time, is evoked by the bright light of the sun, whose rays appear among the clouds. The light catches the ripe, tall stalks of wheat, creating a gentle ripple through the golden field. The bucolic quality of this scene is set into relief by the figure of a peasant playing the bagpipe and women baking bread peacefully under a deeply rooted, leafy tree. People work in this Arcadian world, but their labor seems blissful. They harvest joyfully to the accompaniment of music, their bodies moving harmoniously, in a dance of sorts, as they bind sheaves. The warm, soft colors of the sheaves, corresponding to the hues of the harvesters' attire, add to the idyllic atmosphere. This, Poussin seems to intimate, is nature and humanity at their best.

Ruth's figure, like all the human figures in this painting, is minute. The Bible, as we have seen, provides no details about Ruth's appearance so it is left to the artist to envision what she looked like. In the world of Poussin's *Summer*, the fact that Boaz approaches Ruth has nothing to do with physical attraction. Ruth's face is somewhat strange looking, deliberately antithetical to standard notions of feminine beauty.[10] Her dark complexion may be an indication of her foreign origin, but it could just as well reflect the deep shade of the tree nearby. However one chooses to interpret Ruth's complexion, her attire is not foreign. Like all the other figures in the painting she is dressed with the kind of clothing that ever since the Renaissance has been considered "biblical" or "classical." To the extent that her clothing differs from that of the other female reapers, it is because of Ruth's modesty (some of the other women have looser dresses and bare shoulders) and the blue color of her skirt. Ruth's blue attire intimates that she is akin to Mary. Blue marks Mary's celestial qualities, and as the most expensive color of the artist's palette it symbolizes sacredness.

That Ruth is something of a Mary figure in this painting is made even more palpable through her gestures. Her face and hands express gratitude and wonder on receiving the unexpected bounty, resembling those of Mary in visual adaptations of the annunciation scene. Boaz, accordingly, plays a double role: he is both the benevolent field owner and the angel who announces the forthcoming birth of the redeemer. In Poussin's own painting of the annunciation from 1657, we find similar gestures, with a similar mélange of wonder, majesty, and humility. The redemptive dimension of *Summer* is further augmented by the sun rays that burst out through the clouds and by the castle in the background, denoting the coming of the Davidic, messianic dynasty. Redemption is set at a distance, but the signs of its approach and the bountifulness of the field offer a hopeful vista of future events.[11] The team of horses trampling on the grain, executed in the style of the triumphal arches of ancient Rome, adds a classical touch to the victories that await the descendants of Ruth and Boaz.

Poussin's mingling of scriptural and mythological elements is pervasive. Ruth is not only affiliated with Mary but also with Demeter, or Ceres (Demeter's Roman counterpart), who is often represented in classical art with a bundle of sheaves in her hands. The story of Demeter and her daughter Persephone is well known. While playing in a field of flowers with the daughters of Oceanus, Persephone is abducted by Hades, the lord of the underworld. Agonized, Demeter revenges herself for the loss of her daughter by forbidding the grain to grow, causing a famine. Zeus intervenes and demands that Hades let Persephone go. Hades feigns obedience, but he secretly gives Persephone a sweet pomegranate seed to eat, knowing that this would force her to return to the underworld for four months every year. Demeter rushes every spring to meet her daughter, and upon their happy reunion restores fecundity to the land.[12] This myth is particularly relevant for Poussin's series, given that it conveys the Greek and Roman perspective on the changing of the seasons. The shadow of Hades (or Pluto) is only implied in *Summer*, but it takes center stage in the last painting of this series, *Winter*, where the Deluge is represented as a mixture of the Last Judgment and the pagan underworld.

A true follower of Virgil, Poussin often records the imprint of death in his Arcadian landscapes. Thus he ventures to render Virgil's description of Daphnis's tomb in the fifth eclogue in his memorable *Et in Arcadia Ego* (1638–1640). This painting depicts shepherds on a spring morning who have come to a tomb with the Latin inscription *Et in Arcadia Ego*, "Even in Arcadia, there am I." The "I" here refers to none other than death.[13] There is an ironic contrast between the tomb, the voice of death in the first person, and the idle merriment that the nymphs and swains of ancient Arcadia were thought to embody. In *Summer*, there

Nicolas Poussin, *Et in Arcadia Ego* (1638–1640). Photo copyright
© Musée du Louvre, Dist. RMN-Grand Palais / Angèle Dequier.

is no tomb, but the shadow of death is introduced through the
Demeter-Persephone-Hades allusion and the juxtaposition to
Winter. No season is set alone. *Summer* is the brightest, but it is
followed by *Autumn* and *Winter.* And yet because the paintings,
like the seasons, are presented as a cycle rather than a linear sequence, we are assured that spring and summer will eventually
return.

In shaping his pastoral Ruth, Poussin conveys a deep long-
ing for a better world, where wheat will grow abundantly, work
will be pleasurable, and human kindness will blossom; but at
the same time he does not hesitate to acknowledge the fragility
of his Arcadia. In that, we might add, he is well attuned to the
book of Ruth itself and its profound view of the ineluctable ebb
and flow of human life.

Poussin's *Summer* had an immense impact on subsequent
pastoral works depicting the book of Ruth. Most of the artists

Julius Schnorr von Carolsfeld, *Ruth in Boaz's Field* (1828).
Copyright © The National Gallery, London.

who followed in Poussin's footsteps endorsed his choice and
focused on the encounter between Ruth and Boaz in the field.
Many of these later renditions lack the human depth and commitment to classical motifs that characterize Poussin's painting,
but they have their own appeal and have surely contributed to
the visibility of this trend. Of the numerous paintings of the
pastoral Ruth across Europe, we'll mention two exemplary ones.
The first is by Joseph Anton Koch (1768–1839), an Austrian neo-
classical landscape painter, who closely adheres to Poussin's
Summer.[14] The landscape in his *Landscape with Ruth and Boaz*

(1823–1825) is Austrian rather than Italian, but many of the details remain the same. Ruth kneels before Boaz in the foreground and her blue and red attire is reminiscent of Mary's colors (Mary is associated both with celestial blue and royal red). Cheerful harvesters are seen among the golden sheaves; others seem to be playing more leisurely under a tree in the background. On the hill close by is a castle, Koch's counterpart to Poussin's "Davidic castle" with its promise of future redemption. Here, as in the bulk of the pastoral paintings of the book of Ruth spanning the eighteenth century to the twentieth, Ruth is represented as a rural beauty and is distinctly local (in Koch's rendition she is even blond). A similar interpretive trajectory is evident in the work of the German artist Julius Schnorr von Carolsfeld (1794–1872). In visualizing Ruth's encounter with Boaz, he portrays her as a beautiful maiden, incorporated into a lovely rural scene. In this case, however, we have a closer vista of the fair Ruth (the landscape is more minimal), who does not kneel but rather stands upright with sheaves in her hands. Her look is slightly seductive, but not to the extent of diminishing the sacred aura of her tilted, somewhat Marian face.

JEAN-FRANÇOIS MILLET'S IMPOVERISHED PEASANTS

Poussin continued to exert influence in nineteenth-century French art, but some of his modern admirers sought to carve out new interpretive paths in the fields of Bethlehem. These new trends were in part indebted to the growing erosion of religious dogma and the rise of new perspectives on the Bible in the context of the European Enlightenment. The Enlightenment has long symbolized the rise of secularism, but as the historian Jonathan Sheehan reminds us, religion did not disappear during this period. There is no clearer witness to this phenomenon than the Bible. The Bible did not only survive but even thrived in this "cradle of ostensible secularization." Among those who spearheaded this dramatic hermeneutic shift were the founders of biblical criticism in eighteenth-century Germany. Using new scholarly methodologies, they viewed Scripture as a text whose significance was best deciphered through a historical-philological investigation. In a forceful demystification of the origin of Scripture, they shattered the traditional notion of the Bible as the Word of God, a unified text of divine inspiration, and suggested that it be treated as a composite work, a product of human endeavor, whose intricate history of composition could be examined like that of any other ancient document. Although the opponents of biblical scholarship challenged the piety of its followers, this turn toward history was not anticlerical. It was primarily motivated by a desire to rejuvenate the Bible by transforming it from a book justified by theology to a book justified by culture. By the nineteenth century, these trends had become prominent in French biblical criticism. Ernest Renan's *Life of Jesus* (*Vie de Jésus*, 1863), with its account of the historical Jesus as a gifted human leader, was the most renowned—and the most controversial—within the French scholarly milieu.[15] But this exegetical revolution had a ripple effect in the world of art as well. An increasing number of painters tried to capture the realities of biblical tales in their visual interpretations, though their approaches were highly diverse.

Some two hundred years after the unveiling of Poussin's *Summer*, the French painter Jean-François Millet (1814–1875) ventured to offer a more true to life rendition of Ruth's tale by taking into account the dire conditions of gleaners. Millet was born in the Norman village of Gruchy, the eldest child in a large family of farmers. His parents saw to it that he received a good education, which included the study of Bible and Latin literature, primarily Virgil. Having shown early signs of artistic talent, he eventually received a stipend to study art in Paris. By 1849, Millet had become one of the prominent figures of the Barbizon school of painters, part of a larger European movement toward naturalism in art that made a significant contribution to the establishment of realist perspectives in French land-scape painting. The school took its name from the French village of Barbizon, on the edge of the Forest of Fontainebleau, where many of the artists gathered. The bulk of Millet's paintings were devoted to scenes of peasant life and work in the fields, a world he was familiar with from childhood. His primary objective was to shift the focus of art from the rich and affluent to the backbreaking toil of the French peasantry.[16]

Millet's most pronounced version of Ruth's tale is *Harvesters Resting (Ruth and Boaz)* (*Le repos des Moissonneurs*). Millet worked on *Harvesters Resting* longer than on any other painting and considered it one of his greatest masterpieces. It was, in fact, the first work to garner him official recognition, a second-class medal at the 1853 Paris Salon, the hub of art life in nineteenth-century Europe. Millet chose an episode in Ruth's tale that could easily be yoked to a pastoral framework: the reapers' meal in the field that Boaz invites Ruth to join. Millet's debt to Poussin is apparent in the soft palette, the centrality given to the golden-hued stacks of grain, and the exquisite orchestration of the movement of the sculptural bodies of the reapers. But Millet's admiration for Poussin's work is accompanied by a notable swerve. There is something unrestful in his harvesters' rest. Whereas the peasants have but a modest meal, the huge stacks of grain behind them belong to the landowner. Unease characterizes Ruth's figure as well: her blurred face is cast down shyly, even reluctantly, as Boaz (who is either the landowner or the sharecropper) introduces her to the seated group. Millet's Ruth is not a foreigner—like the harvesters she wears typical nineteenth-century French peasant clothes—but she is still a stranger. She seems to suspect that the harvesters would not be eager to have her join their intimate circle and share their modest lunch. And the harvesters, indeed, seem somewhat suspicious, albeit curious. For Millet, the reapers' meal in the book of Ruth is not quite a joyful, leisurely moment. He highlights

Jean-François Millet, *Harvesters Resting (Ruth and Boaz)* (1850–1853).
Photograph © 2022 Museum of Fine Arts, Boston.

what Poussin and other painters of the pastoral Ruth overlooked: those who glean are among the most underprivileged, and even reapers who attain a slightly higher rank must deal with a tasking job and low pay.[17] While providing a bleaker perspective on rural work, Millet also relinquishes traditional Christian symbolism. His Ruth does not resemble Mary, and no redemptive light or Davidic castle is seen on the horizon. Millet was not a churchgoer, but neither was he a secular artist. His use of religious motifs (many of his paintings are devoted to scriptural themes) represents a modern attempt to redefine the value of biblical tales by calling attention to the realities of everyday life in rural cultures.

Gleaning was a topic Millet would explore in greater detail a few years later in his well-known piece from 1857, *The Gleaners* (*Les glaneuses*). In this painting, he does not refer explicitly to the book of Ruth, but Ruth was still on his mind, in no small part because gleaning was often associated with Ruth in nineteenth-

Jean-François Millet, *The Gleaners* (1857). Photo © Musée d'Orsay,
Dist. RMN-Grand Palais / Patrice Schmidt.

century France. Ruth's tale, in fact, was often evoked in debates
about the laws and practices of gleaning.[18] In many parts of Europe, the biblically derived right to glean was practiced by—
and reserved for—the local poor.[19] In France, in particular, laws
of gleaning have a rich and tempestuous history. Attempts to
regulate gleaning are found as early as the thirteenth century.
Around 1260, Louis IX issued an ordinance forbidding cattle to
enter the fields until three days after the end of the harvest in
order to enable the poorest of the poor to glean. In the eighteenth and nineteenth centuries the state stepped into the picture to ensure that farmers would grant rural paupers their
gleaning rights. Government officials presented it as a moral
imperative and used scriptural texts to reinforce their position.
In addition to the legal corpus on gleaning in Leviticus and Deuteronomy, they relied on the book of Ruth to convey the great

value of the custom. The farmers, however, opposed the government's policy, arguing that the state was merely using them to exempt itself from providing welfare. The debate took on added urgency during the agricultural crisis of mid-nineteenth-century France, which led vast numbers of peasants to migrate to the industrialized cities. As farmers saw their income diminishing at a disturbing rate, they insisted on defining the right of gleaning as their own. More often than not it was the wives of the peasants or harvesters who gleaned (for it was less demanding physically), providing supplemental earnings for their families.[20]

In *The Gleaners*, Millet foregrounds three peasant women gathering leftovers on a partially cloudy harvest day. The poverty of these women is evident in their coarse, simple garments and their strenuous work.[21] The scattered grain glitters against the drab color of the ground, yet we cannot help but realize how meager the leftovers are, and how much effort the women must make simply to live. Their faces are hidden, unidentifiable, implying that they represent a type of destitute people rather than individuals. Each gleaner stands for a different age of womanhood. The youngest gleaner, who wears a blue kerchief, picks bits and pieces of wheat with agility; the middle-aged woman, with a faded reddish kerchief, is less nimble but she too stoops over; and the eldest one, whose kerchief is greyish-brown, can barely bend. Each woman deals differently with the tasking work, but together they create a distinct rhythm of gleaning. Here, as in *Harvesters Resting*, there is a contrast between the scarcity that prevails in the world of the poor and the landowner's huge stacks of grain in the background. The landowner on horseback watches the gleaners from afar, ensuring that the considerable distance between the three women and the bountiful stacks remains.

Millet's debt to the book of Ruth is apparent not only in his attention to the experience of gleaning but also in his choice to

allot agency to poverty-stricken women, who all too often remain invisible. Much like Ruth, Millet's gleaners arouse both
compassion and respect for their determination to struggle for
survival, and their quiet fortitude amid the monotony and rig-
ors of their work. Perhaps the very fact that Millet chose to portray a sense of solidarity between women of different ages also
harks back to the book of Ruth. Although Naomi never gleans
in the field (she may have been too old for such labor), she shares
the experience and benefits from the bundles her daughter-in-
law brings back daily during the harvest season. In both of Millet's adaptations of Ruth's tale, he projects biblical scenes of
gleaning onto the fields of rural France. In doing so, he aspires
not only to highlight biblical details that earlier artists left unrecorded but also to endow the peasants of the Barbizon district
with a biblical aura and a sense of dignity.

When Millet presented *The Gleaners* at the Salon in 1857,
it was largely criticized—deemed suspiciously revolutionary in
spirit. In the aftermath of the Revolution of 1848, critics saw it
as adhering too closely to socialist ideals. But some could appre-
ciate its revisionary power at its unveiling. Théophile Gautier,
poet, journalist, and literary critic, described Millet's painting
as revolving around "three gleaners advancing in line, bent toward the ground, collecting in their tanned hands rare, fallen
shoots of grain, because some Boaz has not recommended to
his harvesters to forget some for these Ruths, who will not be
slipping into the tent of the master in the evening."[22] After the
Salon, Millet, short on money, sold his piece for three thousand
francs—below his asking price of four thousand. After his death,
public appreciation of his work steadily increased (both in Europe and the United States), and in 1889 the painting sold for
three hundred thousand francs at auction. It now resides in the
Musée d'Orsay in Paris as one of the masterpieces of French art.

Why *The Gleaners* enraged nineteenth-century viewers more
than *Harvesters Resting* is an intriguing question. The difference

may be attributed to the fact that in the earlier piece Ruth is un-assuming and is ultimately brought into the community, whereas in the later painting, the three "Ruths" are set apart, neglected by all, in contradistinction to the denouement of the biblical tale. But what also bothered early critics was the fact that des-titute, "ugly" women were set centerstage and allowed to loom large on a huge canvas of 33 inches by 44 inches.[23] These three grand gleaners represented a decisive break with the beautiful, delicate pastoral Ruths who had become iconic in modern art.

Today it is difficult to imagine the resentment and fear that *The Gleaners* initially evoked. For many contemporary view-ers, unfamiliar with the context of Millet's rural paintings, *The Gleaners* seems far from a social critique or a break with artistic conventions. It is often regarded as a pastoral painting due to its soft, harmonious hues, monumental figures, and favorable, even somewhat idealized representation of rural life. But *The Gleaners*, like *Harvesters Resting*, offers a curious mixture of pas-toral and anti-pastoral elements, embodying both a debt to and a departure from Poussin's inaugural, classical landscape of *Sum-mer*. Millet's homage to Poussin in *The Gleaners*, we should add, is also apparent in his choice to regard Ruth's tale as the basis for a broader reflection on the human condition. If Poussin highlights the ebb and flow in Ruth's life, Millet focuses on her resilience in the face of hardships. For Millet, Ruth's gleaning becomes an emblem for the vital need to struggle against all odds in a post-Edenic world where the verse from Genesis—"By the sweat of your brow shall you eat bread till you return to the soil" (3:19)—is only too reflective of the realities of human life and work.

ORIENTAL BEAUTIES

While Millet was searching for Ruth's footsteps in the fields of Barbizon, other mid-nineteenth-century artists sought to render the pastoral gleaner against the "real" biblical landscapes of her life, in the "Orient." Within this new orientalist framework, Ruth is no longer represented as a European local but rather as a beautiful, exotic woman of the enchanting Eastern world. Curiously, although Ruth is now perceived as foreign, she remains local within her own community. She is singled out by her beauty but otherwise blends in with the other Israelites, who, much like her, are presented in Eastern dress. No sweat is seen on the brow of any gleaner or harvester in these paintings. The blissful atmosphere that was evident in classical seventeenth-century renditions of Ruth's tale is reinstated against the backdrop of the pastoral Orient.

The perception of the Bible as an oriental gem, one that is best interpreted in relation to the customs of the East, was first developed in eighteenth-century German biblical criticism. The turn toward history of German Bible scholars was carried out in different ways. While some were immersed in historical-philological investigations, others were determined to contextualize the Bible as the product of the Eastern imagination. Johann Gottfried Herder was undoubtedly the most fervent and famous advocate of the latter approach. In his guidelines for readers of the Bible in *Letters Concerning the Study of Theology* (1780–1781), he offers a succinct formulation of the *Einfühlung* (empathy/sympathy) required for a better appreciation of the Bible's oriental character: "Become with shepherds a shepherd, with a people of the sod a man of the land, with the ancients of the Orient an Easterner, if you wish to relish these writings in the atmosphere of their origin; and be on guard against abstractions of dull, new academic prisons, and even more against all so-called artistry which our social circles force and press on those sacred archetypes of the most ancient days."[24] To fathom the power of biblical writings, à la Herder, we must enter empathetically into the convivial, oriental setting of the folk who created them. Herder's biblical Orient is a pastoral one, which is why he urges us to "become with shepherds a shepherd" as we become Easterners with ancient Easterners. Previous scholarly studies, he claimed, tried to erase the stamp of the rural, ancient Orient and lock scriptural texts within "academic prisons," but such "dull" endeavors must be rejected. The East, in Herderian eyes, is nothing less than essential for the rejuvenation of biblical criticism and, by extension, for the rejuvenation of Western tradition as a whole.

Herder did not write about the book of Ruth, but some of his followers did.[25] In *West-Eastern Divan* (1819), Johann Wolfgang von Goethe depicts the book of Ruth as the Bible's "most lovely small, well-unified work handed down to us in an epic and idyllic form."[26] His brief comment on the book of Ruth as exquisitely "small" evokes the etymology of *idyll*, a term that derives from the Greek *eidyllion*, a diminutive of *eidos*, "little picture." Goethe's Ruth thus embodies a blend of Greek pastoral and oriental cultures. Inspired by Herder (as he openly admits), Goethe regards the book of Ruth, alongside the Song of Songs, as a precious, idyllic relic of the ancient Orient.

In the mid-nineteenth century, popularized adaptations of Herder's ideas were to be found across Europe and the United States in biblical encyclopedias, in newly designed family bibles, and, above all, in the highly popular genre of Holy Land travel literature. European and American literary markets were flooded with narratives and diaries of travelers to the Holy Land. Such literature set out to capture the "original," oriental qualities of the Bible by offering tours of the region that laid bare the biblical traces inscribed in it.[27] Peasants in Ottoman Palestine were presented as an ethnographic window on to the past, or as living embodiments of biblical characters and customs. Traveling in the Holy Land was synonymous with walking between the lines of an illuminated Bible, where the locals, through their daily practices, reenacted the text and the accompanying images.

The book of Ruth was among the privileged biblical texts

in Holy Land travel literature. Every pilgrim to the Holy Land, from Late Antiquity on, would necessarily visit Bethlehem, to view the birthplace of Christ. But in the nineteenth century the fields surrounding Bethlehem were also regarded as a tourist-pilgrim attraction. By witnessing contemporary peasants harvesting and winnowing visitors could, as it were, travel back in time and envision the enchanting harvest scenes of Ruth's tale.

Seeking the oriental dimension of the book of Ruth became a common practice in the world of art as well. Among the French orientalist artists who chose to paint Ruth was Hughes Merle (1822–1881). Mostly forgotten today, Merle was a frequent exhibitor at the Paris Salon. His work, typically sentimental, often depicting scenes of familial bliss or religious import, circulated widely in Europe and was also bought by American collectors during the last decades of the nineteenth century.[28]

Merle's Ruth, painted in 1876, is an oriental beauty. She stands upright and gazes at an unseen point in the distance with dreamy eyes. Her complexion is dark and her eyebrows are black and quite thick. She wears Eastern garb (as do all the other figures in the painting) and is adorned with a necklace that matches the reddish plaid scarf wrapped around her waist. The long scarf tied to her head, resembling those of Arab women, blows backward in a soft swirl toward Boaz and his workman, who are talking in the background (about Ruth, we may assume). Other reapers are seen working by Boaz in the yellowish semi-arid fields. On the far right one can see Bethlehem, now imagined as a village or town in the Middle East rather than as a lofty European castle.

Much like other pastoral Ruths, Merle's ancient gleaner holds sheaves in her hands, but her alluring appearance discloses a new interpretive line. A seductive quality was already noticeable in Julius Schnorr von Carolsfeld's Ruth, but Merle goes a step further in painting the ancient gleaner in a semi-transparent blouse through which viewers could have a glimpse

Hughes Merle, *Ruth in the Fields* (1876). Image courtesy
of the Art Renewal Center® www.artrenewal.org.

of her well-shaped breasts. Though fanciful, Merle's painting
highlights an element in the biblical text that had not received
much attention in earlier visual interpretations: the curious
blend of modesty and seductiveness that characterizes the ancient gleaner.[29]

Merle offers his audience a holy biblical figure who is at
the same time a voluptuous, oriental woman. He combines two

major lures of the orientalist East: sex and the sacred. And he does so while maintaining a sense of propriety, making sure that his paintings could be hung on the walls of the abodes of his numerous admirers (as they certainly were). In the wake of Edward Said's influential book *Orientalism*, we have become aware of Westerners' tendency to project their fantasies onto the East.[30] But we should also bear in mind that when dealing with the representations of biblical figures in art, we are by definition in the realm of the imaginary. We may prefer the paintings of Poussin and Millet for their artistic distinction and complexity, but they too are the product of European imaginings. Envisioning Ruth as a Mary, a Ceres, or an impoverished French peasant is by no means coming closer to the "real" Ruth.

Moving from the world of paintings to that of illustrations, we discover that French orientalism also produced modest-looking oriental Ruths. Illustrated Bibles were meant for the family as a whole, and accordingly illustrators avoided any kind of sexual innuendo that would make their work offensive to Victorian readers. The most renowned Bible illustrator of the nineteenth century was Gustave Doré (1832–1883). Doré's artistic talent was apparent early in life. During his teens, he produced thousands of caricatures for different periodicals and became the highest paid illustrator in France. Later, in the 1850s, he delved into the realm of belles-lettres, creating engravings for books by great writers, among them François Rabelais, William Shakespeare, Victor Hugo, and Charles Dickens. In the following decade, Doré turned to the Bible. His illustrations for the grand *Bible de Tours*, published in 1866, were immensely successful and have been reproduced ever since worldwide.[31]

Doré's Bible illustrations were extolled by his contemporaries for their historical accuracy and reliance on the new archaeological findings in the Middle East. The theologian and critic Émile Le Camus wrote in *Le Contemporain* that Doré, "taking everything he could from the most recent discoveries regarding the architecture, customs and mores of the Assyrians, Jews and Egyptians, gave his scenes a local color that will make them eternally true."[32] Today we may smile at the comments of critics who attributed authenticity to Doré's work, but at the time and for many decades following, his illustrations were regarded by both religious and increasing numbers of secular readers as admirably vivid reconstructions of biblical realities.

In Doré's visual interpretation of Ruth's gleaning in the fields, she appears in a typical oriental costume, but a very modest one. None of her clothing is transparent or even semitransparent. Her hair and body are fully covered as she peacefully squats to collect a few sheaves while holding a bundle on her bent knee. Ruth's beautiful, radiant face is majestic, and her gaze is directed, dreamily, toward the ground. Immersed in her own world, she seems to be oblivious to the men behind her. Neither Boaz, who asks about the new gleaner, nor the young reaper, who carries a large bundle of sheaves while turning back to look at her, are within Ruth's chaste field of vision.

Doré is a master of visual staging. While the virtuous, tranquil Ruth is lit by a spotlight as the center of attention, we can see commotion in the background, created by several men on camels. It is not clear why these camel riders crop up in the midst of a harvest scene, but they surely highlight the oriental character of the backdrop while adding a dramatic element to the picture. One of the men, with a staff in his hand, leans forward on his camel. He seems to be waiting for the climactic moment of the drama, as if he were aware that the next episode in the show will begin once Boaz approaches the beautiful gleaner who has aroused his attention. And we too, as viewers, are invited to join, with the advantage of facing the stage and seeing the entire drama unfolding before our eyes.

The Bible offers no information about Ruth's appearance. But this omission did not keep artists from Late Antiquity to modern times from depicting her in their work. Perhaps, to the

Gustave Doré, *Ruth in the Field* (1866). ✪ Wikimedia Commons.

contrary, the lack of specific information gave them the freedom to imagine her in whatever way they deemed appropriate.
We noted that Ruth acquires a central position in Western art
after she becomes a pastoral gleaner in Poussin's *Summer*. But
the image of the pastoral Ruth is by no means static: it changes
as we move from one cultural and artistic context to another.

Poussin advanced the merging of Ruth's tale with classical pastoral motifs, but some of his nineteenth-century followers embraced other possibilities. Millet combined pastoral elements with anti-pastoral elements in his attempt to draw nearer to the actual living conditions of gleaners. And orientalist artists such as Merle and Doré transferred the pastoral to the East, portraying their Ruths in exotic clothing. In most of these visual renditions of Ruth, she is cast in traditional feminine roles. She is resolutely modest, and even when she becomes more seductive, she is still chaste. Another predominant tendency is to imagine her as beautiful, although both Poussin and Millet insist on breaking with conventional standards of feminine beauty. And however submissive Ruth may seem in many instances—kneeling before Boaz or bending down—she is often seen as embodying the unique power of a Mary, a Ceres, or, in more earthly terms, a resilient impoverished peasant.

In its emphasis on local scenes, the pastoral interpretive trend is responsible for the common reading, even today, of the book of Ruth as anything but a migrant's tale. While overlooking migratory aspects, the pastoral trend has the advantage of shedding light on the idyllic qualities of Ruth's tale. The most compelling visual renditions of the pastoral Ruth call attention to the exceptionally peaceful atmosphere of the book of Ruth and the admirable human goodness that prevails in the fields of Bethlehem. At the same time, like Virgil's *Eclogues*, they also remind us of some of the more dire features of human life and invite us to imagine a better future.

5

---◆·◆·◆---

The Zionist Pioneer

THE ZIONIST RUTH shares much in common with the pastoral gleaners of European art. She too is a beauty, often oriental looking, who appears with a bundle of sheaves against a backdrop of glistening fields. But unlike her European precursors, the Zionist Ruth is not quite a gleaner, nor even a typical peasant, but rather a bold pioneer who takes part in the renewal of Jewish agriculture in the Land of Israel.

The Zionist Bible was, in many ways, the heir of the European Enlightenment Bible. Israeli society in the twentieth century was more invested in secularism than eighteenth-century Europe. Yet this greater commitment to secular paradigms did not prevent Zionist exegetes from defining their national project via the Bible and passionately seeking new ways to reformulate the significance of the biblical text. The Zionist pioneers of the early twentieth century had Bibles in their rooms. The Bible, in fact, served as their bridge between the land they had long imagined and the land they found upon arrival; it was vital to their primary effort to transform the strange geography of Ottoman Palestine into a new national home.[1] Later, with the establishment of the State of Israel, the Bible's cultural centrality was reinforced. In a letter of 1953, David Ben-Gurion, Israel's first prime minister, claimed that with the rise of Zionism the "Bible shines in its own light" (ha-tanakh zore'ah be-'or 'atsmo) and need not be obscured by later rabbinic interpretations.[2] "The books of the Bible," he insisted, "declare the glory of Israel. As to the glory of God—that is declared by the heavens."[3] Rather than viewing the Bible as God's book, as the rabbis did, Zionists viewed it as a book whose power lay in its historical account of the unique bond between the people and the land.

The book of Ruth acquired a highly privileged position in early Zionist culture.[4] In Zionist eyes, Ruth's tale was to be embraced with enthusiasm, for it provided a valuable precedent— a story of a happy return to the pastoral landscapes of Zion. Ruth's migration was recast as a blessed homecoming, an aliyah (literally, "ascent"). Much as early Zionists defined their own migration to Palestine as an ascent, so too they imagined Ruth as an archetype of the ola (ascender). In a sense, Zionist exegetes adopted the definition of Ruth's migration in the biblical text itself as a return: "And Naomi came back, and her daughter-in-law with her who was coming back from the plains of Moab" (1:22). They too, like the biblical Ruth, regarded the Land of Israel as home, although they had never set foot in it before. What made the book of Ruth all the more compelling was its vivid gallery of agricultural scenes—precisely what the first pioneers and later the kibbutzniks adopted with enthusiasm. Ruth's story was often recited or even dramatized in kibbutz ceremonies of Shavuot. It enabled kibbutzniks to reenact biblical scenes of harvest and to regard their agricultural work as the true continuation of everyday life in ancient Israel.

The Zionist rendition of Ruth as a pastoral pioneer flourished across different media, but over time, it lost its monopoly and other perspectives emerged. In the early 1920s, S. Y. Agnon, one of the founders of modern Hebrew literature and a Nobel laureate, ventured to reread Ruth as a quintessential stranger while pointing to the delusional aspects of any homecoming. For many decades no one followed in Agnon's footsteps. But by the end of the twentieth century, and particularly at the beginning of the twenty-first century, the preoccupation with the migratory aspects of the book of Ruth have increased significantly in both Israeli literature and art. If early Zionist exegetes tended to ignore Ruth's foreign origin and the agonies of acculturation, now the darker facets of her life were set into relief. This exegetical shift too has had an impact on the practices of Shavuot. In current Tikkunim of Shavuot—a new Israeli version of the Kabbalists' nocturnal vigils during the holiday of Shavuot—Ruth's tale is often evoked as a migrant's story and is discussed in relation to the pressing problems faced by immigrants, refugees, and minorities in contemporary Israel.

THE BEZALEL SCHOOL OF ARTS AND CRAFTS

In tracing the shifts in the afterlives of Ruth in the Israeli context, we begin with the adaptations of the leading artists of the Bezalel School of Arts and Crafts, the renowned institute of early Zionist art. Ephraim Moses Lilien, who assisted Boris Schatz in founding Bezalel in 1906, was the first to transform Ruth into a visual Zionist emblem. Born in Drohobicz, Galicia (then part of the Austro-Hungarian Empire), in 1874, he later moved to Germany, where he resided until his death in 1925. He is often considered the most prominent Jewish artist to be associated with art nouveau or Jugendstil, a style of art, architecture, and decorative arts that emerged at the turn of the twentieth century. Lilien visited Ottoman Palestine several times and had much influence on the first generation of Bezalel artists.

Lilien's black-and-white illustration of Ruth of 1912 was one of many he produced for *Die Bücher der Bible*, the first Bible fully illustrated by a Jewish artist in the modern period.[5] In shaping his Ruth, Lilien tapped into the deep reservoir of French art: from Poussin he took the redemptive vision of Ruth's tale, from Millet the image of Ruth as a powerful, hardworking woman, and from Doré the orientalist approach and dramatic staging. And yet, while relying extensively on this European heritage, Lilien created a strikingly new image of Ruth, one that had never been seen before on any canvas. His Ruth is an audacious pioneer, a *halutza*, who is engaged in hard work in the fields and is willing to face any hardship that lies ahead. Her dream of the future is revealed in the minute sketch of a castle that looms above the dark background. It calls to mind Poussin's distant castle in *Summer*, but here the architecture is more oriental and the sought-for redemption is of distinctly Zionist bent. Lilien imagines Ruth as working toward the foundation of a new Jewish state—a modern, Davidic kingdom that is to be built not via divine will but through human agency. In many ways, this strong-willed Ruth is a female counterpart of Theodor Herzl, the legendary Zionist visionary of the Jewish state. In Lilien's well-known 1901 photo of Herzl, the Zionist leader is seen standing on the balcony of Basel's Hôtel Les Trois Rois during the Fifth World Zionist Congress, gazing forward intently, as if envisioning the emergence of the new state of the Jews right there and then. Lilien endows Ruth with a similar gaze. Looking forward and slightly up, she is the harbinger of a dramatic transformation in Jewish history. Ruth's elevated vision is highlighted by the upward thrust of her noble posture. She seems larger than life as she walks through the unusually tall and bountiful bundles of sheaves that surround her.

It is nighttime—not the traditional midday of the classical pastoral. Lilien chooses to add to the work in the fields elements from the nocturnal scene on the threshing floor. He is well attuned to the boldness of Ruth as she steps into the night alone.

Ephraim Moses Lilien, *Ruth* (1912). Wikimedia Commons.

Her goal, as Lilien reimagines it, is not to seduce the sleeping Boaz (who is altogether absent) but rather to assume the role of an agent of redemption, to follow her own bright vision of a new beginning, even though much remains unknown on this dark night whose dim stars are barely noticeable.[6]

If Lilien's pioneer Ruth creates a storm among the bundles of sheaves, it is not only because of her national initiative but also because she seems to be breaking with traditional gender roles. Women are not expected to go outside at night without a male companion. What makes her all the more exceptional in gender terms is the oriental scarf wrapped around her waist that resembles a tallit, the Jewish prayer shawl, which was worn solely by men in Lilien's day. To be sure, Lilien is not trying to fashion a new practice of women wearing a tallit (analogous to the custom embraced today by some Reform Jewish women). Rather, he is suggesting that Zionism has paved the way for a more egalitarian world, where women can partake in nation-building and where strenuous agricultural work is not necessarily a prerogative of men. The actual division of labor among the pioneers during the first waves of Jewish migration to Palestine was less radical. In many cases, women who wanted to work in the fields were relegated to the traditional feminine roles of cooking and cleaning, and eventually child care.[7] But Lilien was not preoccupied with the realities of pioneer life. He was far more interested in the imaginary Zionist pioneer woman and in casting the biblical Ruth as her formidable foremother.

In imagining Ruth as a pioneer, Lilien was also eager to define his own work as a vehicle for pioneering, to present himself as a visionary Jewish artist who could provide his people with images of their own. Reflecting on an exhibition of young Zionist artists organized by Lilien in conjunction with the 1901 Congress, Martin Buber writes, "For thousands of years we [Jews] were a barren people. We shared the fate of our land. A fine, horrible desert sand blew over it and blew over us until our sources were buried. . . . We were robbed of that form which every people takes . . . the ability to behold a beautiful landscape and beautiful people. . . . All things . . . whose forms are forged through art's blessed hands, were something foreign to us . . . which we encountered with an incorrigible mistrust."[8] Buber speaks of the exhibition as a refreshing antidote to the disastrous neglect of art during the long years of Jewish exile.

From Buber's perspective, Lilien spearheaded an aesthetic re-naissance that was no less vital than the foundation of a Jewish state: the barren "desert" of Jewish art was in dire need of cul-tural pioneers who could turn the wasteland into verdant artis-tic landscapes, teeming with new life.

To advance this new Jewish art required a reassessment of the Orient. In keeping with a predominant Zionist trend, Lilien regards the Orient not merely as an exotic region but also as a key to understanding the origin of Judaism.[9] Lilien is as obliv-ious as European orientalist painters to the living conditions of peasants and shepherds in Ottoman Palestine, but unlike his precursors he views the local Arabs as resembling his own an-cestors. Jews were often ridiculed in European culture for their dark features—until the nineteenth century, they were, in fact, the paradigmatic representatives of the Orient in European eyes—but now the Eastern look could be endorsed as part of the new Jewish identity that was blossoming in the Land of Is-rael. Lilien's dark-haired Ruth and his dark-haired and bearded Herzl seem to be proud of their non-European hues. Other de-tails are relevant as well. Even in placing the huge bundle of sheaves on Ruth's head (rather than in her hands), evoking the common practice of women in Arab villages, Lilien intimates that the East ultimately offers better models for new Jewish women than the West.[10]

The most elaborate visual interpretation of the book of Ruth was provided by the Bezalel artist Ze'ev Raban (1890–1970) in an illuminated edition of the book of Ruth, published in 1930. Born in Poland, Raban later studied at various European art academies, among them the École des Beaux-Arts in Paris. In 1912 he left Europe and joined the Bezalel School in Jerusalem, where he became a leading painter, decorative artist, and illus-trator. He illustrated a number of biblical books. Alongside his work on Ruth, he published illustrated editions of the Song of Songs (1923) and the book of Esther (1947). His illustrations of these biblical women have had a lasting impact in Israeli culture and still circulate widely.[11]

In Raban's most iconic, colorful illustration of Ruth, she is portrayed as standing upright with a copious bundle of sheaves on her head. Raban pays tribute to Lilien's illustration while opting for another take on the theme. Adopting the more idyllic European representations of Ruth, he casts her against the backdrop of delightfully cultivated fields on a bright sunny day. No shadow of the nocturnal episode on the threshing floor complicates the pastoral setup. What is more, Raban harks back to more conventional configurations of femininity. Though Raban's Ruth follows in the footsteps of Lilien's Ruth in carrying a substantive sheaf on her head, the work itself seems to be effortless and delicate. She is a curious cross between a Zionist pioneer and an enticing oriental princess.[12] The light-blue silk dress that she wears and the golden, oriental ornamental decorations on her chest and waist endow her with royal glamour. The new Zionist "kingdom" is represented not only via the dim houses of Bethlehem in the distance but also through Ruth's sumptuous clothing. Raban may have been familiar with the midrashic commentary on Ruth as the daughter of Eglon, king of Moab, but his choice to portray the ancient gleaner in royal attire is primarily meant to mark her role as the mother of a new dynasty in the Orient.

Raban, like Lilien, adds a Zionist touch to European orientalism, but given his symbolist style, he veers more toward the legendary symbols of Eastern culture. On closer look, we realize that Raban's royal Ruth is brought into our world on the wings of imagination—or rather on a magic Persian carpet. With a dreamy, innocently seductive gaze, she emerges through a pointed oriental gate that serves as the carpet's frame. On both sides of the gate we notice lush, decorative palm trees (a typical trope of orientalist art) whose fruit clusters are purplish, seemingly a blend of dates and grapes. The trunks of the two palm

Ze'ev Raban, *Ruth* (1930). Image courtesy of the
Center for Jewish Art at the Hebrew University of Jerusalem.

trees, embellished with exotic flowers, serve as the gate's two
regal columns. Raban is fond of introducing biblical scenes
through oriental gates. In the poster he designed circa 1929 for
the Society for the Promotion of Travel in the Holy Land titled
"Come to Palestine," he provides a visual interpretation of the
renowned verses of Song of Songs 2:11–12 that are inscribed as
its base: "For, lo, the winter is past, the rain is over and gone;
the flowers appear on the earth; the time of the singing of birds
is come, and the voice of the turtle is heard in our land."[13] The
viewers are invited, as it were, to enter the golden oriental gate
that frames these amorous sights, to enter the Zionist spring,
and to join the pastoral world of the shepherd and shepherdess

who tend their flock in the green hills above the Lake of Galilee and Tiberias.[14] Passing through Ruth's gate or flying on her magic carpet leads us to a summer scene of harvest rather than to spring pastures, but the effect is quite similar. For Raban, both the book of Ruth and the Song of Songs are essential for the formation of a riveting, pastoral Zionist Orient, where the tilling of land and the herding of sheep could be carried out peacefully by the returning descendants of the ancient Israelites.

At the bottom of the frame of Raban's illustration of Ruth, an enchanting gazelle is seen crouching. Raban uses this stock image of Persian miniatures to underscore the mythical, oriental character of the scene but also to enhance the link between Ruth and David. In the final illustration in Raban's edition of the book of Ruth devoted to the concluding genealogy, we see King David, dressed in oriental clothing, under a leafy tree in pastoral fields playing on his harp, while a gazelle crouches by his left side and a majestic deer with tall, fine horns leaps to his right. Here the mythical animals are not set in the external frame but cross over into the biblical scene itself, as if to indicate that legends could become a reality. Ruth and David do not appear together in Raban's illustrated version of Ruth's tale, but the deep affinity between the two is made visible by recurrent symbols. In the 1950s biblicism of Ben-Gurion, the biblical David will be hailed as a brave warrior, but for Raban he is primarily the musician-poet-shepherd descendant of the pastoral Ruth.

Some of the photographers of the Bezalel School were also involved in advancing images of the Zionist pastoral Ruth. One such photographer was the director of the photography department at Bezalel, Yaacov Ben-Dov (1882–1968).[15] In one of his staged photos of around 1918, we see a Bezalel student dressed in oriental garb posing as Ruth, with a bundle of sheaves in her hands. Ben-Dov was not the first to produce staged biblical photographs. Ever since the invention of photography in the mid-

Yaacov Ben-Dov, *Woman in Biblical Scene* (Bezalel Student Dressed as Ruth) (ca. 1918). Copyright © The Israel Museum, Jerusalem.

nineteenth century, an increasing number of European and American travelers to the Holy Land brought their cameras with them. While recording the holy sites along the way, they also, occasionally, dressed up in biblical costumes and took photos of their performative adventures in Ottoman Palestine. Ruth was a favorite choice for women. The collection of early twentieth-century photographs shot by the American Colony photography team includes a series of photos of a Western woman (either a tourist or a member of the colony) who was photographed with Ruth-like Arab costumes against the backdrop of wheatfields in the vicinity of Jerusalem or Bethlehem.[16] In Ben-Dov's Zionist version of such staged photographs, the significance of the pose changes. The Bezalel student who plays Ruth stands for the new woman nation-builder who strives to fulfill the Zionist dream.[17] Ben-Dov is an artist, not a producer of souvenirs. His Ruth is lit from below with a special light that adds grandeur to her image. She does not face the camera, smiling at her relatives, but rather gazes backward, toward the remote patches of trees at the distance. Among the trees in the background, we notice a blurred edifice which is the old building of the Bezalel School. The new Bethlehem or the new temple of Jerusalem is now located in the pioneer art world of Bezalel's artists.[18]

When Herder urged Bible readers to "become with shepherds a shepherd" and with "Easterners an Easterner," he could not have anticipated the passion with which Zionist exegetes would seek to cross into the world of the ancient Orient and merge with the pastoral heroes and heroines of the biblical past. But for Bezalel's artists and photographers, "passing for" the ancient Israelites and retrieving their supposedly ancient, oriental culture seemed indispensable for the revival of the Bible and, by extension, for the rejuvenation of Jewish culture in the Land of Israel and beyond.

S. Y. AGNON'S *IN THE PRIME OF HER LIFE*: UNCANNY LOVES

Though art was the primary habitat of the Zionist pastoral Ruth, she also appeared occasionally in the realm of modern Hebrew literature. In fact, the Zionist perception of the book of Ruth was invented in Avraham Mapu's proto-Zionist novel *The Love of Zion* (1853), the first novel written in Hebrew and

one of the literary peaks of the Jewish Enlightenment. Like
Ruth and Boaz, Mapu's lovers meet in the fields of Bethlehem.
Their love, however, is not merely a personal matter but also
a national event—an individual relationship that embodies the
resurgence of a new love for Zion in the pastoral Orient.[19] The
most notable follower of Mapu was Jacob Fichman, whose
1920 poem "Ruth" offers an exemplary Zionist perspective on
the pastoral Ruth. Filling the gaps in the biblical text, Fichman's
Ruth ruminates as she strides *be-mish 'oley ha-layla*, "on the
paths of the night," toward the threshing floor. Walking bare-
foot in the "foreign land" that has welcomed her, Ruth per-
ceives each step on this path as part of a "holy covenant with a
new homeland." She recalls her fascination with Mahlon's "foreign tongue" (*niv zar*) back in Moab, where she already felt as
"the daughter of his land" (*bat artso*). But now, on her way to
the threshing floor, Ruth is ready to embrace a new love—for
Boaz—while committing herself to the idyllic land she has always regarded as her own.[20]

But the most intriguing Ruths of modern Hebrew literature take us far beyond idealized Zionist landscapes and into
estranged worlds and estranged loves. The notable forerunner
of this darker interpretive line is S. Y. Agnon. Agnon was born
in 1887 in the town of Buczacz in Eastern Galicia. After the
Kishinev pogrom in 1903, he became involved in Zionist circles
in Buczacz, and in the spring of 1908 he immigrated to Palestine. Like many other members of the Second Aliyah, he became nonobservant while taking part in the thriving new literary scene in Jaffa.[21] In 1912, Agnon moved to Germany, where
he stayed for several years. On his return to Palestine in 1924 he
chose to live in Jerusalem and to become observant yet again.[22]
Oscillating between the religious and secular worlds, Agnon
held a remarkably perceptive and unorthodox approach to both.
He was as ironic toward traditional exegesis as he was toward
Zionist biblicism.

In *Only Yesterday* (1945), Agnon depicts a group of art students of Bezalel who see in Sonya—a new immigrant, or ola, from Russia—a perfect embodiment of Ruth, the ancient gleaner. Although Sonya is something of a "Northern" type (the students cannot but admit), they find her compelling as a model and justify their choice by claiming that "Ruth the Moabite also had something northern in her, for the redhaired David came from her."[23] Agnon offers an amusing debunking of the insistence of Bezalel artists on endowing biblical figures with an "authentic," oriental look. Were it not for the aesthetic exigencies of Bezalel, after all, the students in *Only Yesterday* would not have had to invent a rationale for the relevance of other hues to Ruth's portrait.

Agnon's interest in the book of Ruth and its Zionist reception, however, did not begin with *Only Yesterday*. His most intricate and elaborate exploration of Ruth's tale is to be found in the renowned novella *In the Prime of Her Life* (*Bidmi yameah*), published in 1923.[24] The Ruth-like narrator of the novella, Tirtza, does not walk with sheaves of barley in the fields of Bethlehem nor is she a pioneer building a new nation. She lives in a small town in Galicia, Buczacz—or Shibush as Agnon called it—and leads a very domestic, bourgeois life, typical of well-off Jewish families in the early twentieth century.[25] The one exceptional activity in Tirtza's world is her writing. She is not only the narrator of the tale but also its author (the only female narrator and the only female author in the Agnonian corpus). Tirtza writes in the biblical Hebrew characteristic of writers of the Jewish Enlightenment, but has no intention of becoming a Zionist.[26] Her writing remains detached from the surrounding eastern European community much as it remains detached from Zionist endeavors.

In *In the Prime of Her Life*, Agnon offers a highly nuanced modernist revision of the book of Ruth, in which moments of self-estrangement and ambivalence in the biblical text are intensified in bold strokes. Ruth's tale is reimagined primarily via the relationship of Tirtza and her mother, Leah. While casting Tirtza in the role of a dislocated Ruth, Agnon envisions Tirtza's mother as an acutely morbid Naomi. "I went out full, and empty did the Lord bring me back" (1:21), cries the biblical Naomi to the women of Bethlehem as she bemoans her dire state. Tirtza's mother does not protest against God (or anyone else for that matter), but she suffers from an acute sense of emptiness that is never alleviated. And whereas in the book of Ruth, Naomi eventually seems to be more willing to accept and acknowledge Ruth's love, her Agnonian counterpart remains incurably indifferent.

Tirtza opens her tale with a memorable elegiac tone (beautifully captured in the recording of Agnon reading it), depicting her mother's untimely death and the melancholy years that preceded it.[27]

> My mother died in the prime of her life. She was barely thirty-one years old. Few and harsh were the days of her life. She sat at home the entire day and never stirred from within. Her friends and neighbors did not visit, nor did my father welcome guests. Our house stood hushed in sorrow, its doors did not open to a stranger. Lying on her bed my mother spoke scarcely a word. But when she did speak it was as though limpid wings had spread forth and led me to the hall of blessing. How I loved her voice. Often I would open her door just to hear her ask, Who's there? . . . Her illness, a heart ailment, bowed her life down.[28]

Tirtza harks back to her childhood, recalling her childish attempt to draw her mother's attention by opening the door. "Who's there" her mother would ask, and Tirtza could pretend for a moment that her mother had noticed her and could take her under blessed, maternal wings. Her mother may have seemed a merciful nurse (*achot*) to outside observers, but in fact she was the patient, a melancholy mother who could take care of no one, not even her daughter.

Despite her mother's indifference, Tirtza wishes to merge with her in every possible way. She could have declared with the biblical Ruth: "Do not entreat me to forsake you, to turn back from you. For wherever you go, I will go. And wherever you lodge, I will lodge. . . . Wherever you die, I will die. . . . So may the Lord do to me or even more, for only death will part you and me." But death does not part Tirtza from her mother. Quite the contrary—her mother's death only kindles Tirtza's need to merge with her. Tirtza spends the rest of her life trying to step into her mother's world, so much so that she insists on marrying Akavia Mazal, the lover whom her mother could not marry.[29] The levirate law seems today a relic of the past that has no significance in current times. But in Agnon's translation of it into modern terms it becomes relevant once again, recast as an emotional drive to preserve familial continuity, the objective in this case being to commemorate the deceased mother while realizing her unfulfilled dreams.[30] Agnon's modification of the levirate law is closer to the biblical text than it may first seem. Even in the book of Ruth, as we have seen, the implementation of the levirate law is meant not only to rescue Mahlon's name from oblivion but also—and perhaps even more—to fill the void in Naomi's life.

Tirtza seeks to continue along the road her mother could not take, to mend past wrongs, but she ends up creating new distortions.[31] In Agnon's novella, the book of Ruth blends with Ecclesiastes 1:15—"the crooked cannot turn straight" (*me'uvat lo yukhal litkon*)—for no distortion can be fully repaired (even one of the dogs in the tale is called *me'uvat*, distortion). If Leah was forced to follow her father's choice and marry the rich Mintz instead of Mazal, the love of her life, Tirtza is determined to marry for love. And yet, in embracing her mother's amorous choice and seducing Akavia Mazal, the man who could have been her father, Tirtza drifts into an unsettling, incestuous realm. There is no biblical or civil law that Tirtza and Mazal violate by marrying, but psychologically the attraction to a father substitute can be as disconcerting as literal incest. Agnon does not hesitate to emphasize the incestuous shadows in Ruth's tale, but he does so with a Freudian touch. Although Agnon took pleasure in denying the fact that he read Freud, his oeuvre is undoubtedly indebted to psychoanalytic theory.[32] In this case, he explores the power and dangers of incestuous drives while considering the ways in which they inevitably introduce an element of estrangement in the midst of our very homes.

At the end of *In the Prime of Her Life*, the pregnant Tirtza is about to give birth to the child her mother could not have with Mazal. Tirtza would have liked, as it were, to be like Ruth, whose son, Obed, is placed at Naomi's bosom. But Tirtza's mother is dead, and the incestuous dimension of her cravings now looms large and weighs upon her in ways she finds difficult to bear. On one wintry night, Mazal comes to her and sings a lullaby while embracing her. Her father, in turn, takes out a pair of slippers and a red cap—presents for his future grandson—imitating a child's piping voice. Both speak of the baby to be born, both treat Tirtza as a child of sorts. Commenting on this moment, Tirtza writes, "I behold the two men and long to cry, to cry in my mother's bosom. . . . My father and my husband sit at the table, their faces shining upon me. By dint of their love and compassion, each resembles the other. Evil has seventy faces and love has but one face." Tirtza's words call to mind the memorable opening line of Tolstoy's *Anna Karenina:* "All happy families are alike; each unhappy family is unhappy in its own way." Agnon provides an ironic variation. Here a supposedly happy family is miserable in its own unique way. The bewildered Tirtza now realizes, more clearly than ever before, that her husband is something of a father and that her greatest wish remains to find shelter in her mother's bosom. Writing, she admits, is her only "solace." It assuages the loss and brings her closer to a sense of reparation and maturation. On approaching motherhood, on feeling "the child within," growing "from day to day," Tirtza ventures to plunge into the story of her life and record its unmistakable distortions, mingled as they are with her ever-vital cravings to mend the past.[33]

In Agnon's oeuvre, individual loves are often intertwined with collective loves, or, rather, they offer a meditation on broader cultural phenomena.[34] The invitation to think in national terms about the amorous bonds of *In the Prime of Her Life* is embedded in Agnon's choice of names. Leah is one of the biblical matriarchs, and "Akavia" derives from the name Jacob, the name of the nation's founding father. But since Agnon's Leah is also something of a Rachel (the beloved matriarch dies in the prime of her life), the entire biblical nexus of Leah-Rachel-Jacob hovers in the background. This legendary triangle from Genesis, however, is inextricably connected to the book of Ruth. In the closing scene of the book of Ruth, the elders bless Ruth as a new matriarch who is destined to follow in the footsteps of her notable precursors—Rachel and Leah—in "building" the house of Israel (Ruth 4:11).

But what happens, Agnon seems to ask, to those who seek to rebuild the house of Israel in modern times? *In the Prime of Her Life* is, among other things, Agnon's ironic response to the Zionist privileging of Ruth as an emblem of redemptive homecoming and acculturation within the old-new pastoral settings of the Land of Israel. Characteristically, Agnon probes both the charms and the delusional aspects of Zionist biblicism. Is such a return to biblical times possible? What makes it so enticing? Can one actually return, after so many centuries away, to the Land of Israel and reenact biblical scenes without creating new distortions? How successful can this modern attempt for the *tikkun*, repair, of exile be?[35]

Agnon veers dramatically from the visions of Mapu and his followers. If there is any love for Zion in *In the Prime of Her Life*, it is as dislocated and unsettling as are the individual loves. Dislocation seems to be inescapable in the Agnonian world—whether one lives in Galicia or in Palestine. There may well be something fundamentally distorted about diasporic life in Shibush (a name whose meaning is "distortion"), but the return to the land of the Bible is far from a clear-cut cure.[36] Peculiar amorous declarations in this novella are performed against the *mizrach* (the ornament that marks the East as the cherished direction of prayer in traditional Jewish homes), but is the actual return to the Orient any less disorienting? What Zionism seems to overlook, Agnon intimates, is the extent to which the aliyot, the waves of "ascent," are actually waves of immigration—and as such embody all the restlessness and ruptures of migratory life. The book of Ruth for Agnon thus becomes a rich source for a consideration of the lingering sense of estrangement even when homecoming is at stake.

MICHAL BEN-NAFTALI'S QUEER MOABITE

Agnon was a lone voice in his subtle reading of Ruth. The predominant tendency up until the last decades of the twentieth century was to continue to embrace Ruth as a national emblem and celebrate her tale as a blissful story of idyllic homecoming. By the 1970s, however, Israeli biblicism had undergone some notable changes. For a nation no longer in the making, as Anita Shapira points out, the need to fashion a national epos via the Bible was no longer paramount.[37] Secular Zionists seemed to have lost interest in the Bible. But from the 1980s on, new interpretive trends emerged in Israeli culture, introducing modes of reading the Bible beyond national agendas. Among the most fascinating new perspectives that became more visible in this period were feminist ones. As an exceptional biblical text in which women loom large, the book of Ruth acquired a new kind of cultural visibility. In Lilien's illustration of Ruth and in Agnon's *In the Prime of Her Life* we noticed a certain break with traditional gender roles, but these reassessments were partial and were not set within a feminist framework. It would take a few more decades before full-fledged feminist renditions of the book of Ruth appeared.

The beginnings of feminist responses to the book do not lie in the Israeli context. The first scholarly feminist reading of Ruth's tale was provided by the American biblical scholar Phillis Trible. In *God and the Rhetoric of Sexuality* (1978), Trible offers a groundbreaking reading of Ruth as a story that defies predominant patriarchal notions, both in its foregrounding of female characters and in its unprecedentedly positive representation of a close friendship between women. Many more feminist readings appeared in the 1980s and 1990s. This feminist scholarly world was by no means homogenous. The perception of Ruth's tale changed over time and varied widely across disciplines. Initially, the emphasis was primarily on gender issues, but later feminist readings sought to broaden the discussion and address Ruth's position as doubly other—both a woman and a Moabite. The observations of Julia Kristeva on Ruth in *Strangers to Ourselves* (*Étrangers à nous-mêmes*, 1988) had much resonance. "Ruth the foreigner," writes Kristeva, "is there to remind those unable to read that the divine revelation often requires a lapse, the acceptance of radical otherness, the recognition of a foreignness that one might have tended at the very first to consider the most degraded. This was not an encouragement to deviate . . . but an invitation to consider the fertility of the other."[38] But there were other notable approaches. In her 1997 article on Ruth as a "model emigrée," Bonnie Honig, a political feminist theorist, provides a critique of Kristeva's approach.[39] Rather than viewing the book of Ruth as representing an exceptionally

favorable view of a foreign woman and of otherness, Honig underscores its underlying ambivalence. From her perspective,
Ruth is a migrant woman who was treated as a surrogate mother
by an unwelcoming Israelite community. We should also note
the 1994 volume of essays *Reading Ruth: Contemporary Women
Reclaim a Sacred Story*, edited by Judith A. Kates and Gail Twersky Reimer, which offers responses to Ruth's tale by Jewish
novelists, poets, psychologists, and scholars. Some of the essays
in this volume endorse a feminist-queer outlook on the book of
Ruth and see in the relationship of Ruth and Naomi a homoerotic bond.[40]

From the 1990s on, these diverse feminist trends were becoming apparent in Israeli culture—both in scholarly circles
and in contemporary Israeli literature. It is against this backdrop that Michal Ben-Naftali writes her version of Ruth. Ben-
Naftali (b. 1963) is a leading contemporary Israeli writer, essayist, and translator, who has played a major role in advancing
queer-feminist literature in Israeli culture. In addition to Ben-
Naftali's commitment to questions of gender, she has been an
advocate of French deconstruction. Thanks to her numerous
translations, the writings of prominent deconstructionists such
as Jacques Derrida, Julia Kristeva, and Maurice Blanchot are
now available in Hebrew. But deconstruction for Ben-Naftali is
not merely a separate scholarly realm. She continually crosses
borders between fiction and deconstructive theories, as she fashions a blend of both worlds.

In 2000, Ben-Naftali published her first book, *Chronicle of
Separation: On Deconstruction's Disillusioned Love*, whose opening section is a narrative by a highly alienated Ruth—not only
a Moabite but also a lesbian.[41] In many ways, Ben-Naftali is as
far as one can get from Agnon—a secular, feminist-queer writer
who is fond of French theory. But curiously, when Ben-Naftali
sketches Ruth's life in *Chronicle of Separation*, she too portrays

her as a dislocated narrator and writer. In Ben-Naftali's rendition, however, the narrator explicitly regards herself as a Ruth who ventures to rewrite her tale:

> I read in the scroll that was named for me and feel at times I know nothing beyond what is written in it, and also that what I know has not been written there at all. You found yourselves a way to circumvent my silence, to trample my loneliness. I hardly speak, speak too little, and so do you, who honed an art of silence that lends itself to an infinity of interpretations. I must write it anew, this scroll, for the first time, as there is no signatory, writer, or judge who has the authority to redact the synapses of the private, minute memory that are heaped and meshed inside me.[42]

Ben-Naftali's Ruth is determined to record her "real" life—all of her memories, however private and minute—as a rebuttal of the silencing of her voice in the biblical account. Far from being a Zionist pioneer or a nation-builder, she sets herself apart from the collective "you" of the people of Bethlehem and their God, resenting the yoking of her story to "the familiar narrative." There are, of course, many lacunae in the biblical text (part of the Bible's renowned "art of silence," as the narrator puts it), but the silences surrounding her life, she insists, are not reflective of an aesthetic stance but of censorship.

What the biblical authors could not bear to mention, we discover, is the true character of the love between Ruth and Naomi. It comes as no surprise that the key text in queer readings of the book of Ruth is the oath on the road. Often cited in matrimonial ceremonies of lesbian couples today, this oath has been regarded by LGBTQ communities in the past few decades (primarily in Israel and in the United States) as an ancient acknowledgment of the value of homoerotic bonds. Ben-Naftali too regards the oath on the road as a climactic scene. It is there that the love between Ruth and Naomi flourishes and where the two destitute widows find much solace in each other. And yet *Chronicle of Separation* offers an intriguing twist. The outburst of love on the road turns out to be a fleeting episode of bliss. Once the two women reach Bethlehem, Naomi is determined to dissociate herself from her daughter-in-law. Ruth's love for Naomi gradually becomes a disillusioned love.

In chronicling the story of their separation, Ruth imagines at one point what would have happened had they ventured to write a scroll together: "If only we could have written this scroll together, mingling each other's mother tongues, biblical expressions and slang, slight words and solid ones. Had we written together your talk would have become coupled with mine, realizing our shared potential to create, be fruitful." But then she recalls the inescapable tensions: "Our language, however, was never the same language. I spoke Moabite. You spoke Hebrew. And when I started to speak Hebrew I stopped speaking the language of my mother and my people, adopting your language. I was wholly foreign to you, even before becoming foreign to the obligations of a Hebrew woman in Bethlehem."[43] The gaps between them, apparently, were not only cultural and linguistic. Even when Ruth relinquishes Moabite and adopts Hebrew as her language, speaking and writing in a foreign tongue in an attempt to draw Naomi nearer, she is rejected.

The tale Ben-Naftali's Ruth ends up writing (on her own) bears a resemblance to Margaret Atwood's *The Handmaid's Tale*. Ruth records, in painful detail, how Naomi manipulated her love by sending her to the threshing floor to seduce Boaz. And then, when Ruth gives birth to Obed, the child is transferred to Naomi's bosom, "anchored by the law." Following the guidelines of the people of Bethlehem, Naomi joins them in demanding, "Make us a child and then go."[44] As a daughter of a nation that was born through sin, through incest, Ruth was expected to mend and redeem and then head elsewhere.

In teasing out the hidden ambivalences of Naomi's conduct

in the biblical text and probing their psychological ramifications, Ben-Naftali is primarily indebted to Kristeva, whose observations are cited occasionally. Kristeva's *Strangers to Ourselves* is of special importance, not only because of its reading of Ruth but also because of its detailed consideration of self-estrangement. In the lyrical opening of the book, Kristeva writes, "Strangely, the foreigner lives within us: he is the hidden face of our identity, the space that wrecks our abode, the time in which understanding and affinity founder. By recognizing him within ourselves, we are spared detesting him in himself."[45] Going with Kristeva beyond Kristeva, Ben-Naftali renders the episode on the road as a period in which Ruth and Naomi were capable of sensing and accepting the estranged within themselves. Their blissful enmeshing, however, is shattered when Naomi ceases to embrace Ruth's strangeness and starts to detest her queer Moabite daughter-in-law.

Ben-Naftali's story ends where it begins: on the road. Lonely and deserted, Ruth sits at a roadside inn. Dreamily oscillating between memories of past times and fantasies of future encounters, she wonders what would happen if Naomi were to show up, suddenly, from a corner of the inn and join her. She may be disillusioned, but her yearning to renew their bond never diminishes.

A queer reading of Ruth would have been unimaginable in the context of early Zionism and even many decades later. But in contemporary Israel, with the growing impact of the LGBTQ community, such readings have an audience. What is more, the question of cultural diversity is a pressing issue. Israel is no longer a community of *olim*, but rather a nation-state with non-Jewish minorities, alien residents, and refugees. In flaunting Ruth's foreign origin, contemporary Israeli writers and artists do not mean to condemn her as a failed convert. To the contrary, the migratory dimension of her tale, as far as they are concerned, requires an empathetic reconsideration.

ADI NES'S GLEANERS

Reconsiderations of Ruth are evident in the realm of visual art as well. The most renowned image of the ancient gleaner as a renegade migrant in contemporary Israeli art is Adi Nes's 2006 staged photograph of Ruth and Naomi, one of fourteen photos that make up his series *Biblical Stories*. Adi Nes (b. 1966) is widely regarded as the leading fine-art photographer in Israel. His work has become internationally recognized for the bold and emotive way in which it confronts controversial issues in Israeli society—most notably in his 1999 staged photo of Israeli soldiers sitting along a table, cast in postures that resemble those of Jesus and the apostles in Leonardo da Vinci's *Last Supper*. Like da Vinci's apostles, the soldiers are devoted disciples of a belief system but also its victims.

In *Biblical Stories*, Nes transports figures from the Hebrew Bible to scenes depicting contemporary homelessness.[46] The biblical characters that ignite his imagination are primarily the foreigners, the renegades, and the outcasts—from Hagar, Esau, and Job to Ruth and Naomi. And even when he stages photos of leaders such as Abraham and David, they are presented in their most vulnerable and forsaken moments. As in earlier series, such as *Soldiers* (1994–2000) and *Boys* (2000), Nes produced the *Biblical Stories* series through painstaking preparations. Rather than choosing professional actors, he usually conducts extensive searches for his models on the internet or by word of mouth. And like a film producer, he scouts locations, selects costume designs, and then photographs the resulting staged scene. In this respect, Nes's work is indebted to Jeff Wall's "cinematography." His staged photographs, like those of Wall, are the product of elaborate calculation and theatricality, once regarded as foreign to the objectives of photography. Nes further modulates his work by evoking artistic precedents, primarily renowned works of art from the Renaissance to the present. Such references to art history are particularly suitable for his photographic renditions of biblical themes. Taking his cue from European artists who used contemporary models in rendering biblical scenes, Nes does the same in his photographic production. This projection of the past onto the present, for Nes, is closer to what a true interpretation should provide: a vivid casting of biblical episodes in contemporary terms. To highlight his commitment to exegetical license, all the portraits in the *Biblical Stories* series are untitled and the names of the biblical characters appear only in parentheses.[47] The underlying notion is that these photographic afterlives are only tentatively related to the biblical stories that serve as their point of departure. Nes's biblical adaptations are no more fanciful than those of Doré or Raban, but in the postmodern framework of his art, providing a self-reflexive angle on the subjective perspective of the beholder is part of the game.

In *Untitled (Ruth and Naomi)*, Nes plunges into the scene of Ruth's gleaning and reimagines it via a dialogue with Jean-François Millet's *The Gleaners*. Nes's Ruth and Naomi, like their French precursors, are bent forward, immersed in strenuous work that yields little.[48] The different shades of brown in Nes's photo evoke the rustic, soft palette of Millet's painting. And yet Nes is primarily interested in intensifying the anti-pastoral elements of Millet's impoverished gleaners. His staged photograph shows two foreign-looking women dressed in rags picking up dropped onions not from a lush wheatfield but from an unpaved street littered with refuse. The true continuation of Ruth's tale in contemporary Israel and beyond, he intimates, is the story of the homeless migrant workers or refugees who rummage for leftovers at the end of a market day in desolate urban settings. What adds warmth to Nes's somber piece is the humanity of his gleaners. In keeping with Millet's interpretive line, he highlights the admirable resilience of these women in the face of hardship. And he also chooses to add Naomi to the

Adi Nes, *Untitled (Ruth and Naomi)* (2006). Copyright © Adi Nes.
Courtesy of the artist and Jack Shainman Gallery, New York.

scene of gleaning, alongside Ruth, to underscore the moments
of solidarity between the two in the biblical text. Ruth's hair
lock tenderly blows toward her elderly mother-in-law, a hint of
silent compassion. The onions they gather may embody their
unshed tears, but they also indicate that even such a lowly vegetable can be something of a treasure for those who seek life
under impossible conditions.

Nes is also inspired by Agnès Varda's 2000 film *The Gleaners and I* (*Les glaneurs et la glaneuse*). In this film, the acclaimed
French documentary film director introduces us to a remarkable gallery of gleaners whom she meets during her travels across
France: impoverished immigrants who search for food in urban
bins, unemployed laborers in desolate rural provinces, a priest
who cites a 1554 French gleaning edict (based on biblical law)
as he walks through a cabbage field, a literacy instructor who

lives off discarded produce at the outdoor market while criticizing the excessive waste that characterizes consumer culture,
and artists who are keen on recycling. Varda's interviewees
pick odd-shaped fruits and vegetables in the fields, unharvested
grapes and figs, day-old loaves of bread, empty cans, and old
refrigerators. In the first sequence of *The Gleaners and I*, Varda
offers a brief meditation on Millet's *The Gleaners*, but nowhere
in the film does she refer to the book of Ruth. It is left to Nes
to capture the relevance of Ruth's tale to contemporary scenes
of gleaning.[49]

While engaging in a dialogue with French artists, Nes also
responds to pastoral renditions of Ruth in early Zionist art. He
calls into question the biblical visions of Bezalel painters while
pointing to the bankruptcy of socialist ideals in contemporary
Israel. Nes's Ruths are neither pioneers nor oriental princesses,
and their work is not part of Zionist nation-building in the revived Land of Israel. The redemptive possibility celebrated in
the visual interpretations of Lilien, Raban, and Ben-Dov is gone.
There is no Davidic castle or temple in the background to sym-
bolize the rise of the new Zionist dynasty. If Nes's gleaners were
to turn their gaze backward, like Ruth in Ben-Dov's staged
photograph, they would discover only dismal heaps of trash—
plastic bags of different sizes, empty vegetable and fruit boxes.
All of the *Biblical Stories* portraits were shot in deserted areas of
Tel Aviv or Beersheba, where one finds, as Nes puts it, "people
whose identity is being erased by society," cast to the outskirts
of an economic system that barely leaves anything for those
who are on the margins.[50]

Nes grew up in a Mizrahi family (his parents are from Iran)
in Kiryat Gat, a peripheral development town in the south of
Israel. His critique of the orientalist bent of Bezalel art stems
from an ongoing personal concern with the misperception of
Mizrahi culture in early Zionist culture. It is difficult to deci-
pher the cultural background of his two gleaners. They are for-

eign looking in diffuse ways, but their attire and slippers call to mind Mizrahi or Arabic fashions. In this case, however, the Eastern qualities of the staged figures are not recruited as relevant to the refashioning of Jewish identity, but rather as emblematic of those who are marginalized within Israeli society. Nes may also be intimating that not only Mizrahim remain invisible but also the Palestinians, whose plight is all too often overlooked by the Israeli public. His untitled gleaners are thus paradigmatic in diverse ways: they offer a critical perspective on global tendencies while calling attention to modes of discrimination in contemporary Israel.

Nes's perspective differs considerably from that of the founders of Bezalel, but he too, at the end of the day, dives into the biblical text in quest of ways to redefine personal and communal dreams. Nes's staged photograph of Ruth and Naomi is often evoked as representing a new approach to the book of Ruth in blogs and sites devoted to Shavuot.

CONTEMPORARY TIKKUNIM ON SHAVUOT

If you walk in the streets of Jerusalem or Tel Aviv on the eve of Shavuot, you will see hundreds of people dressed in white (the color of the holiday) on their way to different Tikkunim. The custom of nocturnal studies on Shavuot has been carried out ever since the sixteenth century, mostly in synagogues. But in the past two decades it has become a major phenomenon in Israeli culture. To what extent are these new Tikkunim related to the Kabbalistic ones? As we have seen, sixteenth-century Kabbalists in Safed stayed awake all night and fashioned exegetical ornaments for the Shekhinah in preparation for the celebration of the giving of Torah (her wedding day). In contemporary scenes, the practice of staying awake at night and studying has been adopted with enthusiasm, but the content and meaning of these vigils have shifted. In this new context, many cultural institutions in Israel, both secular and religious, hold events throughout the evening and night of Shavuot. A variety of speakers, among them academics, writers, artists, and activists, take part in panels that are primarily devoted to Jewish learning and to pressing problems in Israeli society. The tikkun, the repair, at stake is not mystical but rather cultural and social.

This resurgence of the new ritual of Tikkun Leil Shavuot is reflective of a new openness in Israeli culture to postbiblical traditions. In contrast to the disavowal of rabbinic and mystical exegesis in early Zionism (most adamantly by Ben-Gurion), many secular Israelis in the past few decades have sought to expand their familiarity with the different layers of Jewish tradition. Various secular batei midrash (houses of study), as well as batei midrash in which secular and religious students study together, have appeared in recent years; the most prominent among them is ALMA, a cultural and intellectual center based in Tel Aviv, founded in 1996 by Ruth Calderon.[51] In fact, the current custom of Tikkun Leil Shavuot first acquired considerable public attention through the widely attended events at ALMA. These Tikkunim were at first primarily a secular phenomenon, but they were later adopted by diverse religious congregations across Israel. We should add that the boundary between what counts as secular and what counts as religious has never been as nebulous as it is in contemporary Israel.

What role does Ruth play in these twenty-first-century Tikkunim? She definitely has a place of honor. There are talks, or even sessions, on the book of Ruth in almost every event of Tikkun Leil Shavuot. Many of these talks are devoted to questions of gender and migration or some kind of mixture of the two topics. In 2014, ALMA held a Tikkun Leil Shavuot titled "The Ger, the Stranger, and the Other" (*ha-ger, ha-zar, ve-ha'aher*), using the verse from Ruth 2:11—"To come to a people that you did not know in time past"—as a subtitle. One of the panels called attention to the deplorable living conditions of refugees from Eritrea and Sudan in Tel Aviv while criticizing the Israeli government's immigration policy. In a more recent 2018 tikkun at Shittim Institute, we find a lecture titled "And You Shall Love the Gera [the female stranger]: A Feminist Perspective on the Book of Ruth."[52] Whereas the biblical law in Deuteronomy 10:19 is cast in the masculine—"And you shall love the ger" (the term *gera* does not appear in the biblical text)— here, special attention is given to the predicament of a woman stranger. Though less prevalent, the LGBTQ community also holds vigils on Shavuot, at which the book of Ruth is read, on occasion, from a queer perspective.

In contemporary Israel, images of the pioneer Ruth in pastoral fields still circulate widely, and Ruth's tale is still recited in harvest ceremonies of kibbutzim. But kibbutz culture no longer holds a privileged position, and accordingly the impact of this inaugural Israeli afterlife has waned considerably. In the past few decades, Ruth has become far more visible in her new role as an exemplary migrant woman. Precisely because Ruth is not a local, she now seems to have the power to hold a mirror to her modern Israeli readers, and urge them to consider new possibilities for cultural and social repair.

If Agnon were living today, he would probably provide us with an ironic take on the charms and blind spots of this new scene of tikkun. We can imagine him writing a biting tale about a young popular scholar of Jewish studies, who—not unlike Uriel Shkolnik in Joseph Cedar's film *Footnote* (2011)—makes sure to speak at no less than six different Tikkunim every Shavuot.[53] We can imagine that Agnon would be intrigued by the increased recognition of the darker facets of Ruth's tale, however different in character from his own. We can be sure that, as fond as he was of exploring exegetical endeavors, he would enjoy observing the ever proliferating new lives Ruth acquires in Israeli culture.

6

The American Outcast

WHEN THE PILGRIMS ARRIVED on the shores of America in the seventeenth century, the book of Ruth was not among the biblical texts they projected onto the new landscapes. Verses from Exodus, Deuteronomy, the Prophets, and the New Testament were far more vital to the fashioning of their errand in this new Promised Land. Later, in the nineteenth century, images of the pastoral gleaner circulated widely, but they were mostly reproductions of European paintings or imitations of European art. It is only in the twentieth and twenty-first centuries that Ruth acquires a quintessentially American look. Her emergence on the American stage takes place when she is embraced by leading writers and filmmakers as a paradigmatic outcast whose migratory tale needs to be heard.

Serving as a safe haven for outcasts and immigrants is a foundational American concept. In 1883, the Jewish American poet Emma Lazarus wrote the sonnet "The New Colossus," whose famous lines were later cast onto a bronze plaque and set on the pedestal of the Statue of Liberty:

> Here at our sea-washed, sunset gates shall stand
> A mighty woman with a torch, whose flame
> Is the imprisoned lightning, and her name
> Mother of Exiles. From her beacon-hand
> Glows world-wide welcome . . .
> "Keep, ancient lands, your storied pomp!" cries she
> With silent lips. "Give me your tired, your poor,
> Your huddled masses yearning to breathe free,
> The wretched refuse of your teeming shore.
> Send these, the homeless, tempest-tost to me,
> I lift my lamp beside the golden door!"[1]

For numerous immigrants who came to New York in the late nineteenth and early twentieth centuries, the Statue of Liberty stood as a beacon of hope. But the discrepancy between dream and reality became immediately apparent at the immigration inspection station of Ellis Island, the first stop for all these new arrivals, situated just to the west of Liberty's high-held lamp. The "Mother of Exiles" was not always as welcoming as these newcomers hoped she would be. The question of how immigrants should be treated was a major concern in the American context from the outset, and it remains a pivotal problem today. Beyond the political debates, however, are also cultural ones. The assumption, at least until the 1960s, was that newcomers should be Americanized, should make an effort to join the American "melting pot." But in the past half century, other voices have emerged. Rather than urging immigrants and their descendants to relinquish their cultural past and efface the languages and traditions of their countries of origin, many are recognizing the value of more fluid, hyphenated identities.

As the approach to cultural diversity changed in the United States, so did the definition of American biblicism. In "The

New Colossus," Emma Lazarus evoked Deuteronomy's injunction to love the stranger but did not disclose her own Jewish background or her work as an activist on behalf of Jewish refugees (she assisted Russian Jews who fled pogroms in the 1880s and sought shelter in the United States). Lazarus's goal was to foster a view of the Bible as a vital component of the American melting pot, which is why her biblicism is as broad as possible. In today's world, however, minority groups in America (of diverse Christian and Jewish backgrounds) are far more interested in using the Bible to formulate the unique features of their respective communities. This new approach is in part related to the increasing impact of more secular perspectives. In contemporary America, the Bible is often cherished not as a religious book but rather as a cultural heritage that needs to be revisited and revised.

It is against this backdrop of the shifts in the perception of immigration and the shifts in the Bible's cultural roles that the most distinguished of the American Ruths have emerged. We do not have a plethora of American Ruths; the book of Ruth never acquired the position of a national epic in America. In this respect, the story of Ruth's American reception is considerably different from that of its Israeli counterpart. And yet there are notable similarities. In recent years, both in the Israeli context and the American one, Ruth's tale has become vital for a reconsideration of the lives of outcasts and immigrants.

American culture has produced some of the most intriguing and experimental modern afterlives of Ruth's tale. We shall follow three of Ruth's distinguished advocates: Allen Ginsberg (1926–1997), a founding figure of the Beat Generation and of Jewish American poetry; Toni Morrison (1931–2019), the renowned African American novelist and Nobel laureate; and Guillermo del Toro (b. 1964), the Mexican American filmmaker whose award-winning fantasy films have left a mark on Hollywood. Each of them belongs to a different cultural and religious background. But regardless of the differences, Ginsberg, Morrison, and del Toro have much in common. All three highlight the migratory dimension of the book of Ruth and downplay or even reject the assimilatory aspects of the tale; all three use Ruth's tale as a rich turf for the exploration of the advantages and complications of preserving the cultural heritage of immigrants in American culture; all three are sacrilegious; all three offer captivating exegetical experiments in splitting the figure of Ruth among several characters; and all three are drawn to Ruth in light of their personal stories of migration or those of their families.

ALLEN GINSBERG'S "KADDISH":
"RUTH WHO WEPT IN AMERICA"

One wintry day in November 1958, as Allen Ginsberg walked down the streets of New York's Lower East Side, he suddenly realized that these were the same streets his mother had known as a little girl after she arrived from Russia. On returning to his apartment, he sat down at his desk and wrote the opening lines of "Kaddish (For Naomi Ginsberg, 1894–1956)," an elegy for his mother that would become one of his most renowned poems. Ginsberg had started to work on this poem a year earlier in a hotel in Paris, but could not find the right rhythm. It was only on having this vision of his mother's past as an immigrant that something opened up in his writing.[2]

Naomi Ginsberg was born in 1894 in the small town of Nevel, then part of the Pskov Oblast in Russia. By 1905 the frequency of pogroms in western Russia had pushed the family to leave. They immigrated to the United States and settled, like many other Jewish immigrants of the time, in the Lower East Side.[3] Several years later, the family moved across the Hudson to Newark, New Jersey, where Naomi went to high school and later trained to become a teacher. Shortly after she met Louis Ginsberg, Allen's father, she had a mental breakdown. Many more followed in the course of her life. During her stays in diverse mental institutions, she received increasingly harsh treatments, among them shock therapy (the standard treatment for patients with what was called paranoid schizophrenia) and a lobotomy. She died in 1956. At her funeral, there were not enough men present to make a *minyan* (the quorum of ten male Jewish adults required for public prayer). As a result, the traditional Jewish prayer for the dead, the Mourner's Kaddish, could not be recited.[4] Allen Ginsberg was in Berkeley, California, at the time and was unable to come to the funeral. His poem "Kaddish" is, in a sense, an attempt to compensate for his absence.

The traditional Kaddish is a hymn of praises addressed to God, written mostly in Aramaic with a few Hebrew words. It is delivered as an affirmation of faith in the face of death, though death is never mentioned. The central theme of the Kaddish is the magnification and sanctification of God's name, most notable in the renowned opening line: "May His great name be exalted and sanctified" (*yitagadal ve-yishtabah shmei raba*). In Ginsberg's heretical "Kaddish," however, the name that is most cherished is not "God," but "Naomi." And death does not lurk behind the scenes, it moves to center stage. No dark detail is avoided in Ginsberg's mournful homage to his mother.

In "Kaddish," Ginsberg employs the same long, associative line he had used a few years earlier in "Howl." But whereas in "Howl" he bears witness to "the best minds of my generation destroyed by madness, starving hysterical naked," in "Kaddish," the most personal of his poems, he cries over one particular mad mind: that of his mother.[5] The staccato phrasing, created by abrupt transitions and dashes, is meant, in this case, to capture the sound of sobbing while displaying the shattering experience of mourning. Fragmentary details pour out, incessantly, one after the other. We receive bits and pieces of Naomi Ginsberg's biography accompanied by a plethora of brief references to books, songs, and films that are somehow associated with her.

The book of Ruth has special resonance within Ginsberg's associative flow. At the end of Section II, he depicts his mother as a woman who was once like "the long-tressed Naomi of Bible or Ruth who wept in America."[6] This biblical allusion has much salience given that Ginsberg repeatedly speaks of his mother as "Naomi" rather than calling her "Mom" or "Mother." Although Naomi Ginsberg is primarily a modern counterpart of the biblical Naomi, she also embodies Ruth's miseries: she is both the "long-tressed Naomi" and "Ruth who wept in America." In keeping with the intertwining of the lives of Ruth and Naomi in the biblical text, Ginsberg allows the two biblical women to merge in his mother's portrait. The "long tresses" add a biblical aura to the picture, and the weeping underlies the migratory experiences the two share in common as they enter Bethlehem. In "Kaddish," the hardships of Ruth and Naomi acquire new life through the tears of a later twentieth-century immigrant woman who could not quite find her way in the Promised Land of America.

But Ginsberg's biblical typology extends even further. As one who lovingly follows in Naomi's footsteps wherever she goes, he, too, is a Ruth of sorts. The very inception of the poem, after all, is indebted to Ginsberg's walking where his mother walked, adhering to her route across the Lower East Side. The visceral, rhythmic first lines of "Kaddish" capture the emotional intensity of that moment.

Strange now to think of you, gone without corsets & eyes, while I
    walk on the sunny pavement of Greenwich Village.
downtown Manhattan, clear winter noon, and I've been up all night,
    talking, talking, reading the Kaddish aloud, listening to Ray
    Charles blues shout blind on the phonograph
the rhythm the rhythm—and your memory in my head three years
    after. . . .
Dreaming back thru life, Your time—and mine accelerating toward
    Apocalypse,

the final moment—. . . .

It leaps about me, as I go out and walk the street, look back over my
    shoulder, Seventh Avenue, the battlements of window office
    buildings shouldering each other high, under a cloud, tall as
    the sky an instant—and the sky above—an old blue place.

or down the Avenue to the South, to—as I walk toward the Lower
    East Side—where you walked 50 years ago, little girl—from
    Russia, eating the first poisonous tomatoes of America—
    frightened on the dock

then struggling in the crowds of Orchard Street toward what? (7–8)

As Ginsberg steps into his mother's world, unexpected memories of the past resurface with dreamy force. He begins with
several fragments of the first years of his mother as a little impoverished immigrant girl. Imagining her emotional responses,
he depicts her standing "frightened on the dock" and "struggling in the crowds of Orchard Street," one of the streets of the
Lower East Side. He even records her conviction that tomatoes were poisonous—a common suspicion among Russian Jewish immigrants in the early twentieth century, who had never
seen tomatoes before.[7] But in Naomi's case, migratory anxieties
were enhanced by an inclination toward psychosis.

With striking audacity, Ginsberg goes on to provide a compassionate close-up of the gradual deterioration of his mother's
mind. The poisonous tomatoes were a prelude to many paranoid hallucinations that followed. Some were colored by Communist condemnations of capitalist America (like many other
Russian Jewish immigrants, Naomi was a fervent Communist);
others were closer to home, revolving around different family
members. Ginsberg displays the whole range: "The enemies
approach—what poisons? Tape recorders? FBI?" (18); "I am a
great woman—am truly a beautiful soul—and because of that
they (Hitler, Grandma, Hearst, the Capitalists . . .) want to shut
me up" (26).

The intensity of Ginsberg's devotion to his ill mother and

his eagerness to identify with her are in many ways as exceptional as Ruth's bold clinging to the destitute, melancholy Naomi
on the road between Moab and Bethlehem. No one else in
Ginsberg's family was capable of drawing so close to her—or
willing to try. And yet the poem's somber, modern take on the
book of Ruth cannot but complicate the question of loyalty.
While being deeply committed to his Naomi, Ginsberg is also
something of a failed Ruth. Beset by guilt for deserting his
mother on various occasions, he discloses, with undeniable pain,
the limits of his devotion. After bringing his mother to a rest
home at the age of twelve (at her request), he was haunted by
regret: "I left on the next bus to New York . . . abandoning
her" (15). To top it all, Ginsberg is forever tormented by the
fact that under pressure from the doctors he had signed the pa-
pers approving his mother's lobotomy (his father had left home
by then), an operation that only worsened her condition: "the
lobotomy—ruin, the hand dripping downward to death" (29).

Engulfed by love, guilt, and an acute sense of loss, Ginsberg strives to carve out a new mode of loyalty: a poetic one.
He casts his mother in the role of a strange, glorious muse,
whose teachings need to be cherished and followed:

> O glorious muse that bore me from the womb, gave suck first
> mystic life & taught me talk and music, from whose pained head I
> first took Vision—
> Tortured and beaten in the skull—What mad hallucinations of
> the damned that drive me out of my own skull to seek Eternity till I
> find Peace for Thee, O Poetry— (29)

Ginsberg longs to recall better moments, when his charismatic,
artistic mother taught him much about music and "talk." But
she inspired him no less in her madness. "Tortured and beaten
in the skull," Naomi manages to draw Ginsberg out of his "own
skull," to urge him to explore possibilities beyond the bland
zones of the knowable or fully discernable. Her mad halluci-

nations open up new horizons of a poetic writing that is fragmentary, not always explicable—but always full of vision.

Of the many chaotic visions of his mother, Ginsberg singles out a letter she wrote to him during her last days at the mental hospital, Pilgrim State. The letter was sent to him by a hospital worker and arrived a few days after Naomi's death. It emerged as a voice beyond the grave, a posthumous farewell:

> Strange Prophecies anew! She wrote—'The key is in the window, the key is in the sunlight at the window—I have the key— Get married Allen don't take drugs—the key is in the bars, in the sunlight in the window.
>
> Love,
> your mother'
>
> which is Naomi— (31)

Naomi's cryptic letter is rather nebulous, but Ginsberg embraces it as an oracular guideline. Searching for a key in the window becomes a mystical-poetic code—an invitation to seek light and liberty, even when one is locked in. But Naomi has additional advice of a different bent: "Get married Allen don't take drugs." She sounds, for a moment, like the Jewish mother of stereotype. And yet here these scattered words convey the heartrending love of a schizophrenic mother grasping for some clarity before her death (she could not even recognize anyone in the last years of her life), determined to pass on to her son a bit of beneficial advice. As a gay man and an avid consumer of drugs, Ginsberg cannot possibly follow these instructions, but he does venture to adopt something of his mother's unintentional guidance by incorporating her within his own literary genealogy. He preserves familial continuity not through marriage and offspring but through a literary *yibbum*, a variation on the levirate law: writing the poetry his mother could not write, taking his cue from the remainders of her discourse.

In "Kaddish," for the first time in his literary career, Ginsberg positions himself as both a founding figure of the Beat Generation and the descendant of an immigrant Jewish muse. His mother's dislocations, he admits, have had a ripple effect in his own life. Her Lower East Side is his Lower East Side, her Jewish Russian heritage is his own, much as her weeping and maddened discourse is also his own. Ginsberg never hid his Jewish background, but in his elegy for his mother he displays his heritage more openly than ever before. He goes so far as to use the Aramaic term *kaddish* as a title while inserting snippets from the Aramaic and Hebrew of the traditional prayer in transliteration at different points of his poem. Today evocations of the Kaddish in Jewish American literature are almost expected. This resonant prayer has become the very token of Jewishness in American culture (think of the major role of the Kaddish in Tony Kushner's *Angels in America*, not to mention Leon Wieseltier's *Kaddish*).[8] But when Ginsberg published his poem in 1961, incorporating the foreign words and the rhythms of the Kaddish was an unusual move, all the more so for a Beat poet. The literary critic Hana Wirth-Nesher describes first-generation Jewish American writers, the sons and daughters of immigrants, as often immersed in fashioning "their own distinctive voices by inscribing traces of immigrant speech into their writing, by retaining an 'accent' of ethnicity."[9] In "Kaddish," Ginsberg partakes in this project as he places the then-marginalized languages of Jewish culture at the cutting edge of the American literary canon. And yet while seeking to construct new meanings for Americanness, he is equally invested in reshaping Jewish tradition. His Kaddish is a heretical poem not only because it revolves around Naomi rather than God but also because it endorses other cultural traditions—be they Buddhist teachings or the memorable rhythms of Ray Charles's blues.[10]

In transferring Ruth's tale to the Lower East Side, Ginsberg wants to repair the past and welcome his mother into American culture as a belated home, to turn her into a Beat muse. But this mode of poetic acculturation by no means entails an erasure of her cultural past or the exceptional features of her life. Outcast as his Naomi-Ruth is, there is something about her lack of assimilability that inspires Ginsberg to envision himself as a sacrilegious poet, singing his Kaddish in the wilderness, while declaring, "I am unmarried, I'm hymnless, I'm Heavenless" (11).

TONI MORRISON'S BLACK BIBLE: DISRUPTED GENEALOGIES

Some twenty years after Allen Ginsberg walked through the Lower East Side and saw a vision of his mother as a little immigrant girl, Toni Morrison published *Song of Solomon* (1977), one of the highly acclaimed novels that would eventually win her the Nobel Prize for Literature. *Song of Solomon* sets out to grapple with the different features of the Great Migration, a migration whose tremendous impact on the United States was still largely unexamined in the 1970s. This massive migration of millions of African Americans from the rural South to the urban North in the early twentieth century was primarily a response to economic scarcity and the prevalent racial segregation and discrimination of the southern states, where Jim Crow laws were the norm.[11] Acculturating to life in the North, however, turned out to be far more difficult than expected. The bold move north marked a new beginning for innumerable African Americans, but racism by no means disappeared, and the loss of certain southern customs was deeply felt. Morrison's preoccupation with the story of this major event in African American history has a distinctly personal dimension. Her father, George Wofford, grew up in Cartersville, Georgia. When he was about fifteen, a group of white men lynched two black businessmen who lived on his street. Soon after the lynching, he moved to the racially integrated town of Lorain, Ohio, in hope of finding employment in Ohio's burgeoning industrial sector. Morrison's mother, Ramah Wofford, was also born in the South, in Greenville, Alabama, and moved north as a little girl. Her parents made the move around 1910 after they lost their farm because of debts. Morrison, unlike Ginsberg, does not aim to record the specific biographical details of her parents' lives, but their experiences left an indelible mark on her imagining of the history of a family of African American migrants in the North in *Song of Solomon*.

Song of Solomon is replete with biblical echoes. Having grown up in a Bible-steeped family for whom biblical verses were part of everyday life, Morrison incorporates scriptural texts in all her novels. *Song of Solomon*'s debt to the Bible is already apparent in the title. But in addition to the Song of Songs, Morrison brings in many other biblical texts.[12] Well aware that the African American migrants often construed their migration as a second Exodus—a monumental transition from the Jim Crow South to the Promised Land of the North—Morrison uses the book of Exodus as one of her building blocks.[13] But as a feminist writer who is committed to exploring issues of gender in the context of migration, she also adds the book of Ruth to her biblical network.[14]

Names are pivotal hermeneutic keys in *Song of Solomon*. Many of the characters in the novel bear biblical names. The Solomon of the title is but the first cue: other biblical names follow, among them Ruth, Hagar, Rebecca, Magdalena, and even the peculiar First Corinthians. Morrison showcases the common practice among African Americans of bestowing upon their children biblical names (the novel includes several scenes of such naming), but while doing so she highlights a broader phenomenon. Though the Bible was originally imposed on slaves by their white masters as a condition of bondage, the African American community turned it into a major source of resistance, used to express their own beliefs and travails. Each one of the biblical names in this novel leads us to its scriptural context, calling upon us to consider the strikingly different meanings biblical names and tales may acquire in black culture.

That one of the characters in the novel is called Ruth is a primary invitation to consider the relevance of the book of Ruth to *Song of Solomon*. Morrison's Ruth is a rather miserable embodiment of her biblical namesake, a Ruth whose attempt to assimilate paves her way to no community. As the daughter of an affluent doctor who migrated to the North in the 1930s and became part of the African American elite in a town in Michigan, she is trapped in a world in which the predominant goal is to pass for white (her father goes so far as to bleach his skin). Her situation only worsens when she marries Macon Dead, who had moved to Michigan after witnessing the murder of his father by whites. Like other black southerners who migrated to the North, he is determined to advance his economic standing. Financially speaking, Macon succeeds in embarking on enterprises that his father and forefather slaves in the South could not have imagined, but in many other ways his embrace of the American Dream is disastrous. He is as merciless toward his black tenants as he is toward his own family members. When Macon witnesses his wife sucking (his version) or kissing (her version) her father's fingers upon his death, he is filled with disgust and vows never to have sex with her again. Having lost first her father and then her husband, Ruth Dead becomes even more lonely and desperate.

The story of the biblical Ruth reverberates with special force when Ruth Dead and Pilate, her sister-in-law, conspire to seduce Macon in ways that call to mind the seduction scene on the threshing floor. The free-spirited Pilate was never close to Ruth, but she yields to the plea of her distressed sister-in-law, who is desperate to bring a son into the world. Following Pilate's advice, Ruth puts "some greenish-gray grassy-looking stuff" in her husband's food.[15] It works. In spite of himself, Macon has sex with his wife for four consecutive days. Ruth conceives and later gives birth to Milkman. A family whose last name is "Dead"—a variation on the deadly names of Mahlon (illness) and Chilion (destruction) in the book of Ruth—seems to be doomed from the outset. But through the joint efforts of Ruth and Pilate, life is cultivated in the Dead family tree.[16]

Ruth Dead, however, is not the only Ruth-like character in the novel. Morrison's biblical typologies are forever fluid. She often splits up biblical figures and explores their different facets through diverse characters. What is more, she allows her characters to play the roles of several biblical personae at once. The most captivating Ruth in the novel is actually Pilate. Although Pilate assumes Naomi's task in staging the seduction of Macon, she is closer to Ruth in her unconventional conduct and her unending loyalty to those she loves. Whereas many of the blacks in town aspire to be white, or at least whiter, Pilate is the notable exception: she never tries to change her appearance or hide her blackness. Macon, her brother, regards her as "a regular source of embarrassment" (20). Not only is she unkempt, refusing traditional gendered dressing (a sailor cap pulled far down over her forehead), but she "had a daughter but no husband, and that daughter had a daughter but no husband." Macon is furious at his sister for cutting "the last thread of propriety," but cannot stop her. Pilate moves to the outskirts of town, where she constructs her own kingdom of female outcasts with her daughter Reba (Rebecca) and granddaughter Hagar. The impoverished, marginalized Pilate manages against all odds to make ends meet. In this case, however, survival is made possible not through gleaning but rather by running a small wine house during Prohibition.

Pilate's daring initiatives are instrumental in rescuing Macon's family and keeping her own from falling apart. But she is no less vital to the preservation of cultural genealogies. When Pilate appears at the hospital at the moment of Milkman's birth, she repeatedly sings a song: "O Sugarman done fly away / Sugarman done gone / Sugarman cut across the sky / Sugarman gone home" (5). Incomprehensible at first, this song, we discover later in the novel, is a key to the retrieving of the history of the Dead family, a history that was almost effaced in the course of their migration.

It is left to Milkman to trace the full version of Pilate's song during his journey back south. Reversing the route of the Great Migration becomes vital to Milkman's growth and familiarity with his heritage. When Milkman reaches the southern town of Shalimar, he comes across a group of children dancing and singing: "Jake the only son of Solomon / Come booba yalle, come booba tambee / Whirled about and touched the sun / Come konka yalle, come konka tambee." The song highlights major events in the history of Solomon's line and its recurrent refrain is: "O Solomon don't leave me here / Cotton balls to choke me / . . . Solomon done fly, Solomon done gone / Solomon cut across the sky, Solomon gone home" (306–307). Deeply moved by the song, Milkman realizes that it recounts the story of his own family and sounds just like the "old blues song Pilate sang all the time" (303), except that the children sing about Solomon rather than Sugarman. The full song, as it emerges in the South, reveals an entire genealogy whose founding father is the flying Solomon (a slave called Solomon), who could soar above the agonizing work in the cotton fields and fly back to Africa. On first reading the novel's title we assume that *Song of Solomon* refers to King Solomon's song. But on reaching the concluding episodes it becomes clear that we have expected to find the familiar canonical texts in their recognizable form all too easily.

In Morrison's black Bible, a legendary African slave in the South can assume the position of King Solomon, and preserving the history of his lineage is just as urgent as preserving the traditions of biblical dynasties. As Morrison molds the Bible in her own way, the Song of Songs and the book of Ruth merge.[17] The song the children of Shalimar sing is associated with Solomon, but its themes are closer to those of the book of Ruth.

Rather than offering an amorous dialogue between two lovers, this southern song provides a genealogy and records the anguish created by the ruptures of a family line in dire circumstances. Bringing Ruth and Solomon together may seem strange at first, but we need to bear in mind that they are part of the same biblical lineage: Ruth is, after all, the great-great-grandmother of Solomon.

What makes Morrison's improvisations on biblical texts in the "O Solomon" song all the more enchanting is her debt to black folklore and music. In an interview on *Song of Solomon*, Morrison explains that the novel "is about black people who could fly. That was always a part of the folklore of my life; flying was one of our gifts."[18] Following in the wake of the flying Solomon, Morrison relies both on tales that she had heard and on *Drums and Shadows: Survival Studies Among the Georgia Coastal Negroes* (1940), a compilation of African American folktales, translated from Gullah.[19] In some of these tales, a moment before taking off, the slaves chant the magical words Morrison evokes in her song: "Wa kum kum munin / Kum baba yano / Lai lai tambee / Ashi boong a nomo."[20] In *Song of Solomon*, these African rhythms and chants intermingle freely with biblical elements, forming a vibrant African American blend. Speaking of slave spirituals, Albert Raboteau, a scholar of African American religion, points to their hybrid character, their unique mélange of biblical tales and African styles of singing, dancing, and handclapping.[21] "O Solomon" is, in a sense, a hybrid spiritual—one that is sung while dancing. What is more, like many traditional spirituals, this song has the kind of flexibility that allows it to convey both the experiences of an individual slave or an individual family and those of the black community as a whole. And much like other spirituals, it touches on the greatest miseries, but its lively rhythms do not allow us to sink. If Solomon chooses to fly across the sky in response to the hardships of work in the cotton fields, so can those who sing his song. "O Solomon don't leave me here" cry his enslaved children, choked by cotton balls, but they too seem to be inspired by his courageous determination to break the fetters and fly back home to Africa. The North, Morrison intimates, is not the Promised Land that the migrants of the Great Migration hoped it would be. Africa is their truer home. And yet, she does not advocate a literal return to the African homeland but rather a figurative one: a fuller acknowledgment of the value of African customs and beliefs within American culture.

Milkman is moved by the grand familial history he discovers in the South, and he takes pride in belonging to the "flyin motherfuckin tribe" (332). At the end of the novel, when he flees from Guitar, his close friend and enemy, he ventures to imitate the flight of his grand ancestor and jumps off Solomon's Leap, a cliff on the edge of Shalimar. Morrison deliberately leaves the ending ambiguous—we do not know whether Milkman manages to fly up, or finds his death in the abyss below. Reclaiming the African American heritage his parents relinquished on moving to the North allows Milkman to "ride" the air, but there is much that hinders his flight—from the ongoing racism of both whites and blacks to the scars of slavery and militant black groups such as Guitar's "Seven Days."

There is, however, one redeeming moment just before Milkman's cliffhanger leap. Hit by one of Guitar's bullets, Pilate (who joins Milkman in the final episode of his journey) turns to her nephew and says, "Sing a little somethin for me." Milkman yields to her last request and sings a variation on his aunt's song: "Sugargirl don't leave me here / Cotton balls to choke me / Sugargirl don't leave me here / Buckra's arms to yoke me." After she dies in his arms, Milkman looks at her with love and admiration, noting that "without ever leaving the ground, she could fly" (340). He now realizes that although Pilate is not mentioned in the song he had heard, she is nonetheless a formidable ancestor, whose unique capacity to fly is as wondrous as that of the flying Solomon.[22] The outcast Pilate exits the stage of *Song of Solomon* as a legendary Ruth who even when flying never leaves the ground or her loved ones.

GUILLERMO DEL TORO'S *THE SHAPE OF WATER:*
LOVING AMPHIBIAN HUMANS

Turning from the world of literature to that of film, and from the 1970s to contemporary exegetical scenes, we end with Guillermo del Toro. Whereas Ginsberg and Morrison were children of immigrants, del Toro is an immigrant himself. Born and raised in Guadalajara, Mexico, del Toro moved to the United States in the mid-1990s and within two decades became one of Hollywood's most distinguished directors.[23] On accepting his star on the Hollywood Walk of Fame in 2019, del Toro turned to his audience and declared, with characteristic passion, that there were two important facts about his life: that he was a Mexican and that he was an immigrant. And although he refrained from mentioning Donald Trump explicitly, he did not hesitate to criticize the president's immigration policy: "As a Mexican, receiving this star," he declared, "no gesture right now can be banal or simple." Addressing all immigrants, "from every nation," he went on to urge them to reject "the lies they tell about us" and to "believe in the stories you have inside."[24] Del Toro is close friends with fellow Mexican filmmakers Alfonso Cuarón and Alejandro G. Iñárritu (they are collectively known as the Three Amigos of Cinema). All three have won Academy Awards in the past few years and have contributed to the development of a Mexican American scene in Hollywood.

As for his religious background, Guillermo del Toro was raised Roman Catholic. In a 2009 interview with Charlie Rose, he described his upbringing as excessively "morbid," saying, "I mercifully lapsed as a Catholic . . . but as Buñuel used to say, 'I'm an atheist, thank God.'"[25] Del Toro's familiarity with biblical texts is apparent in his fantasy film from 2017, *The Shape of*

159

Water. It is there, among the different shapes of the water, that we discover a fascinating gallery of cinematic afterlives of Ruth.

The Shape of Water is a film about films. It is primarily a re-make of Jack Arnold's 1954 *Creature from the Black Lagoon,* but also of Henry Koster's 1960 *The Story of Ruth.*[26] From the very first sequence, viewers are called upon to consider *The Shape of Water*'s affinity with *The Story of Ruth.* Elisa, the film's heroine, lives above the Orpheum movie theater, where—the brightly lit marquee indicates—*The Story of Ruth* is currently being shown. The camera first leads us to Elisa's apartment, where she is seen sleeping against a watery backdrop, but then the camera sinks down, wandering through the floorboards and onto the screen in the theater below, zooming in on scenes from Koster's film. For a moment, we do not quite know which movie we are watching: there are recurrent shifts between Elisa's apartment and the voices and images of *The Story of Ruth.*

Koster's *Story of Ruth* was one of many biblical films pro-duced in Hollywood over the years.[27] The American film in-dustry turned Holy Writ into a book to be seen, available to millions of viewers, literate as well as illiterate, for the reason-able price of a movie ticket. It offered a reconstruction of the biblical past that was unprecedented in its mode of realism and power of make-believe. Movies on biblical themes had ap-peared in the silent film era, but the heyday of Hollywood's biblicism was in the 1950s and early 1960s. Although the Bible lost something of its religious aura in modern America, during the Cold War it became an emblem of American superiority. America distinguished itself from the totalitarian atheist bloc of Communist-dominated countries by defining itself as a nation under God. Hollywood saw it as a task to make this difference visible, the outcome being widescreen biblical epics with famous stars, glamorous costumes, and huge sets. The most prominent director of Hollywood's biblical epics was Cecil B. DeMille, whose most ambitious biblical epic and most profitable film was

The Ten Commandments (1956). Among the publicity materials for this film is a drawing of Charlton Heston (who plays Moses) standing beneath the Liberty Bell, his arms stretched overhead, as if holding the enormous bell. The text beneath explains that the verse inscribed on the Liberty Bell—the divine mandate "to proclaim liberty throughout the land, unto all the inhabitants" (Leviticus 25:10)—is taken from the writings of Moses. What this drawing implies is that the United States has now mastered the best strategy of "proclaiming liberty throughout the land": motion pictures. In endorsing the Bible, Hollywood thus strove to add glamour not only to America but also to itself. In a review of *The Ten Commandments*, the American journalist and humorist James Thurber commented that the film "makes you realize what God could have done if he'd had the money."[28]

When Henry Koster ventured to follow in the footsteps of DeMille in projecting a biblical tale onto a wide screen, he chose to produce a film about the book of Ruth. Koster's *The Story of Ruth* is not one of the most successful films of this biblical genre, but it has been viewed by millions since its release and has had considerable resonance.[29] The first part of the film revolves around Ruth's life in Moab. She is imagined as a beautiful priestess of the Moabite god Chemosh who on meeting Mahlon one day realizes that the human sacrifices at her temple are ethically wrong. Ruth becomes doubtful of her religion and falls in love with Mahlon. The two marry, and Ruth embraces Mahlon's God and people as her own. The cruel Moabites are enraged by Ruth's change of heart and send Mahlon to work as a slave at the quarry, where he ends up dying. After the death of Mahlon, Chilion, and Elimelech, Ruth and Naomi journey to Bethlehem. Ruth is first treated with contempt by the people of Bethlehem, who accuse her of being idolatrous, but once she proves to be an exemplary believer in the monotheistic God and (more implicitly) in American exceptionalism, she is wholeheartedly accepted by the community. The final sequence shows the festive, oriental-style wedding of the deeply enamored Ruth and Boaz.[30]

In *The Shape of Water*, Del Toro visits the theater below and explores the earlier layers of Hollywood's biblical epics, but then goes on to build other stories of Ruth above the Orpheum that dismantle the Cold War–infused vision of his predecessors. *The Shape of Water* focuses on the lives of variegated outcasts who are relegated to the margins either because of disability, racial background, sexual preference, or even species: the mute Elisa (played by Sally Hawkins), the African American Zelda (Octavia Spencer), the homosexual neighbor (Richard Jenkins), and the Amphibian Man or creature (Doug Jones). Each of these characters embodies something of Ruth's tale, the most prominent Ruths being Elisa and the amphibian creature.[31] If this were not complicated enough, both Elisa and the creature bear certain features of Boaz as well. In del Toro's fantasy world, biblical typologies are definitely fluid, defying character boundaries, gender boundaries, and even species boundaries.

The most extravagant Ruth of *The Shape of Water* is the Amphibian Man. Needless to say, no one before del Toro envisioned Ruth as an amphibian being. And yet for del Toro, an aficionado of monsters, it is a vital interpretive leap. Monster films in the 1950s (*Creature from the Black Lagoon* among them) do not speak explicitly of immigration, but in many ways they convey Americans' suspicion and rejection of strangers during the Cold War. The monster is the ultimate terrifying stranger, standing for all those who come from foreign countries and seem to threaten the well-being of the American people. But what would happen if we adopted the monster's perspective, asks del Toro. Once del Toro's amphibian creature becomes humane and wondrous, he can merge with Ruth and allow us to view the world from the immigrant's point of view. The bad guys in del Toro's film are the American authorities who have captured the Amphibian Man in South America and then lock him in a government research lab in Baltimore. Failing to see his humanity, they call him "the asset." The Amphibian Man, however, is as fortunate as the biblical gleaner, for he is recognized by a local: Elisa. If he were to ask Ruth's question—"Why should I find favor in your eyes to recognize me when I am a foreigner?" (2:10)—Elisa would express her compassion and admiration through sign language and the peculiar gifts she provides: hard-boiled eggs instead of sheaves.

Thinking of Elisa as a Ruth adds another twist to del Toro's tale. Elisa is not a foreigner, but given that she is mute and can communicate only through sign language, she is something of a stranger as well. The critical theorists Gilles Deleuze and Félix Guattari call attention to the ways in which the literature of minorities undermines the culture of the majority by introducing foreign features and foreign words, weirding the language of the majority.[32] Elisa's sign language is a wonderful emblem of a minority language that offers an estranged version of English. Interestingly, del Toro does not choose to represent particular features of the American Hispanic community (though the creature was found in South America) or to use Spanish as the foreign tongue that hovers in the background. Instead, he opts to invent a more parabolic community of marginalized characters who share a knowledge of sign language and can thus communicate with Elisa.[33]

If Elisa towers above all the other Ruths in the film, it is primarily due to her exceptional boldness—and the phenomenal acting of Sally Hawkins. With feminist sensibilities, del Toro presents Elisa as a "woman of valor," who despite her lowly position as a cleaning woman in the lab designs a daring plan to rescue the Amphibian Man from the water tank where he is kept. In a scene that calls to mind the unflinching female solidarity of *Thelma and Louise*, Elisa and her co-worker Zelda manage to fool their mean, sexist boss Strickland (Michael Shannon) and smuggle the creature out of the facility. Endearingly, Elisa hides him in her bathtub (a magical mixture of the extraordinary and the ordinary), in an attempt to provide the essential aquatic conditions. Elisa's audacity, however, culminates in her unconditional love. How far does she go? All the way. One of the most striking episodes in the film takes place when Elisa and the Amphibian Man make love in the bathroom (not merely the bathtub), after filling it almost to the ceiling with water. The shadow of forbidden sexual relations lurks behind the threshing floor scene in the biblical text, but here del Toro moves beyond incest and dares to flirt with bestiality. And yet there is something so contagious and spellbinding about Elisa's ability to love a fishlike man whom others regard as a monster that we cannot but accept this aquatic love. The innovative visual effects of the many shades of greens and blues along with Alexandre Desplat's soundtrack make the scene all the more dreamy.

In the book of Ruth, the romantic aspects of the bond between Ruth and Boaz are barely represented. This omission does not suit Hollywood. In bolstering the romance in his adaptation of the book of Ruth, del Toro follows Koster's interpretive choices in *The Story of Ruth*. And yet del Toro surely advances another aspect of romance. An interspecies love, in which the local becomes estranged, would have been inconceivable in the context of the Cold War cinema, just as the foregrounding of women's agency and adamantly independent female characters would have been unimaginable.[34] Even the notion of what counts as a happy ending is different. Although Elisa and the Amphibian Man live happily ever after, as the film's narrator assures us in his final comments, they do not lead a conventional terrestrial life but rather cultivate their eternal love in the waters of a Baltimore canal. It is only there, far away from the bullets of Strickland, that strangers can thrive and celebrate their silent sign language. And it is only there that Elisa can miraculously sprout gills and become an amphibian woman. The closing image is of the two happily entwined as they dance in a wondrous marine underworld. Del Toro's vision is bleaker than Koster's, but he does not go as far as Ginsberg and Morrison in using Ruth's tale to explore the ambiguities of migratory lives and loves. His goal, after all, is to produce a "fairy tale for troubled times."[35] Through a romantic fantasy film, he allows us to both face and escape some of the disturbing realities of our era.

Ruth undergoes radical transformations as she moves from Ginsberg's Lower East Side to Morrison's South to del Toro's Baltimore. Even within each of these different worlds, her portrait changes, for she is split among diverse characters. She steps into the lives of a Jewish American schizophrenic woman and a Beat poet; she then becomes an African American recluse and a flying black foremother; and more recently, she ventures to merge with a mute cleaning woman, her African American co-worker, her homosexual neighbor, and an amphibian creature. These different Ruths roam about in strikingly different worlds, but they all represent a break with orthodox visions of Ruth as an exemplary convert. Rejecting assimilation as a cherished value, Ginsberg, Morrison, and del Toro call for a more fluid perception of cultural identities. They want to inscribe something of their Ruths' original cultural backgrounds. To do so, they introduce foreign languages and traditions into the American cultural sphere—from the Aramaic and Hebrew of the Kaddish to the African rhythms and chants of Solomon's song, to the sign language of *The Shape of Water*.

In all these twentieth- and twenty-first-century adaptations, Ruth is set on a pedestal as a quintessential outcast, a beacon of hope for a culturally diverse United States that would be more welcoming toward, or at least less suspicious of, the strangers who arrive on its shores. Such hope remains partial in these rather dark renditions of Ruth's tale—but unmistakably vibrant.

EPILOGUE

———◆◆◆———

Remainders

In my introduction, I noted that to write a biography of Ruth means to become a gleaner. To some extent every biographer is a gleaner who painstakingly culls materials from diverse sources and archives. In Ruth's case, however, the fact that we have but sparse scenes full of lacunae means that to write anything about her life requires the kind of effort that is closer to the task of the gleaner. But above all, Ruth's tale makes us realize the richness of gleaning as a metaphor.[1] To write a biography of Ruth as a gleaner means to follow her model, to venture to find life in remainders, even the most minute.

There is something deeply moving in exploring Ruth's cryptic tale. It provides us with a glimpse of a lost feminine world and reminds us of the many women in biblical times whose stories were not deemed worthy of recording. We would have liked to have a real *book of* Ruth, an entire book that would provide us with many more chapters about other episodes in her

EPILOGUE

life, much as David has the bulk of the copious book of Samuel at his disposal. Ruth, alas, offers us a world of textual scarcity. And yet, the wonder of it all is that after spending much time with the migrant gleaner in the fields, we manage, little by little, to gather way beyond our wildest dreams.

Gleaning from the book of Ruth was our point of departure. The next steps were devoted to Ruth's afterlives and the readers who followed in her footsteps, from Late Antiquity to today. We traced a line of Ruth aficionados: rabbis, Kabbalists, painters, writers, poets, photographers, and filmmakers from diverse cultural and religious backgrounds. We noticed that Ruth offered a voice for those confronting pain and impoverishment, as well as for the pariah, the scapegoat, and the heretic; we saw that she is often evoked as a beacon of hope even when redemption seems tenuous, and that her bold loyalty is admired even by those who regard it as inimitable. In each case, we tried to fathom what happened to the migratory aspects of her life. We discovered that there is no linear development, no neat distinction between premodern and modern adaptations. We find obfuscations of Ruth's Moabite origin and elaborations of her migratory life in both premodern readings and modern ones. The predominant tendency in Late Antiquity was to regard Ruth as a convert and relegate her foreignness to the margins. But in the Middle Ages, within the tomes of the Zohar, she emerges as a Shekhinah whose exilic agonies are set into relief. And when Ruth resurfaces in the context of modernity, she thrives both as a local pastoral gleaner and as a paradigmatic stranger.

Gathering these highly diverse afterlives of Ruth and placing them together creates a riveting collage. Imagine some of the textual and visual images that we have delved into set side by side: the convert on the road; the Shekhinah "brimming with sorrow" on the celestial threshing floor; the pastoral gleaner in paintings from Nicolas Poussin's *Summer* to Ze'ev Raban's il-

167

lustration; the dislocated Tirtza at the closing scene of S. Y. Agnon's *In the Prime of Her Life* seeking solace in her writing; Michal Ben-Naftali's queer narrator waiting for Naomi at a desolate roadside inn; the homeless urban gleaners in Adi Nes's staged photograph; Ginsberg's migrant mother "who cries in America" on arriving as a little girl from Russia; Toni Morrison's Pilate who can fly without leaving the ground; and Guillermo del Toro's Elisa and her amphibian lover dancing in the deep. These different afterlives reveal much about their own times and the hermeneutic and aesthetic choices of their producers. And yet at the same time they all shed light on the multifaceted portrait of the biblical Ruth, enriching its admirable human depth.

If Ruth's charm never seems to diminish, it is also because of the rituals that commemorate her tale. We noted that the book of Ruth is part of Jewish liturgy, read annually on Shavuot, the Feast of Weeks, in Jewish congregations across the world. But the relevance of Ruth's life to Shavuot has been reinterpreted time and again over the centuries. Through exegetical acrobatics, the rabbis of Late Antiquity drew an analogy between Ruth's conversion and the conversion of the people of Israel as a whole on receiving the Torah at Sinai. Medieval Kabbalists took their cue from the rabbis and added a mystical twist. In their nocturnal vigils of Tikkun Leil Shavuot, they strove to repair the exilic condition of the Ruth-like Shekhinah and to celebrate her union with the blessed Holy One on the day of the giving of Torah. Another radical shift occurred some five hundred years later in the context of early Zionism. In Shavuot ceremonies of the kibbutzim, the agricultural significance of the holiday as a holiday of harvest was restored and Ruth was celebrated as a precursor of the Zionist woman pioneer. In the past two decades, we witness another swerve in Israeli culture. In the contemporary version of Tikkun Leil Shavuot, Ruth's tale has had a major role in discussions on various topics, from the pressing problems of immigrants and refugees to feminist critiques.

This current trend is also apparent in Ruth's American reception. In the 1980s, Tikkun Leil Shavuot observances, with special attention to the question of social justice, were held by liberal Jewish American communities. In recent years, such Tikkunim have become more visible given that many Jewish community centers across the United States have adopted the custom.[2] The spirit of social and cultural tikkun is also noticeable in posts devoted to Shavuot on websites of Jewish American organizations. Consider the recent website of Women of Reform Judaism, on which Shavuot is hailed as the only Jewish holiday that positions a story of a woman at the center. Women of this community are invited to form study groups during the holiday and reflect on Ruth as a woman of valor. They are also encouraged to embrace the ethical heritage of the law of gleaning in assisting the hungry in soup kitchens and homeless shelters in their vicinity.[3] The website of the Hebrew Immigrant Aid Society reflects a similar stance vis-à-vis Shavuot. Founded in 1881 to assist Jews fleeing pogroms in Russia and eastern Europe (Emma Lazarus was among its first distinguished volunteers), HIAS now seeks to provide aid to all who have fled persecution. In a 2016 blog for Shavuot, Rabbi Rachel Grant Meyer calls for a reading of the book of Ruth as a tale that can teach us much "about welcoming the stranger" in our midst.[4] Beyond the contours of Shavuot, we should mention one more contemporary ceremonial scene at which Ruth's tale has been evoked: lesbian weddings. In many weddings of lesbian couples, of diverse religious and cultural backgrounds, Ruth's oath on the road is cited as an ancient vow of women's love. The primary goal of these ritualistic uses of the book of Ruth is to redefine communal lives and activities by reclaiming this ancient text—and they certainly have succeeded in doing so.

What will the next chapters of Ruth's biography look like?

We can predict that Ruth's migratory dimension will continue to be pivotal in her future afterlives. Migration is one of the most pressing problems of our time, with political implications we must reckon with daily. In recent decades, we have witnessed millions of migrants and refugees seeking shelter and sustenance in other countries—be they migrants from Central America at the United States–Mexico border, Syrian refugees in Germany, African refugees in France and Israel, or Ukrainian refugees across Europe. And disputes over immigration policies are among today's most heated debates. But migration concerns us not only in the political sphere. It touches on our personal lives in profound ways. Many of us are either immigrants ourselves or children and grandchildren of immigrants, or some combination thereof. With its remarkable human depth, Ruth's tale invites us to explore the ripple effect of migrations that continue to reverberate in us as we find ourselves, time and again, wandering between cultures and languages.

The fascination with Ruth's story of migration, as we have seen, is also indebted to the fact that it is a woman's tale. With the increased interest in gender differences in accounts of migration, we can assume that Ruth's plight will continue to serve as a primary touchstone through which to explore the specificities of the experiences of women migrants.

And perhaps, particularly in light of the COVID-19 pandemic and the unfolding climate crisis, the practice of gleaning will resurge, with fresh urgency, as a major means of survival, and Ruth will be regarded as a notable precursor. In an article in the *New York Times* of July 6, 2020, titled "Meet the Gleaners," Rachel Wharton reports on a growing number of gleaner groups across the United States in the wake of the pandemic and the ensuing economic crisis. The gleaners in this case are volunteers, of different ages, who collect surplus produce from local farms and then donate it to those unable to feed their families. Evoking the book of Ruth as an early, cherished model, Wharton claims that the "age-old tradition" of gleaning has been adopted in recent years with a new emphasis "on supporting local agriculture, reducing waste and improving the nutritional quality of food in hunger relief."[5] We can imagine that this merger of agricultural activism and environmental awareness will only increase in the coming years, and in turn it will be represented in new literary and artistic adaptations of Ruth's tale. But alongside these more foreseeable adaptations, we can also predict that sooner or later Ruth will emerge in another garb altogether, one that we cannot begin to imagine at the moment.

Before parting, I would like to look at two more snippets of Ruth's afterlives that have remained on my desk, or rather in my computer files. What better way to end this biography of Ruth than with a few precious remainders that did not quite fit within the preceding chapters? Leftovers come in different sizes. I begin with a minuscule commentary in Ruth Rabbah on Naomi's condition just before leaving Moab. She is described as being a "remnant of remnants" (*sheyarei shyarim*).[6] With but two words this midrashic gem poignantly depicts her disintegration at the lowest point of her life. The choice of metaphor— remnant of remnants—is not without significance. It provides not only a piercing image of the melancholy Naomi, who has lost her husband and two sons, but also an implicit portrait of Ruth as a figurative gleaner. From the rabbis' perspective, Ruth's hesed toward Naomi is displayed, as it were, both in the sheaves she provides and in her commitment to pick up the pieces of her mother-in-law's broken life.

The more sizable leftover I would like to explore is John Keats's "Ode to a Nightingale" (1819). Keats, a leading poet of English Romanticism, offers one of the most memorable darker renditions of Ruth's gleaning. In fact, this is the first modern rendition of Ruth as a quintessential stranger. To tackle Keats's rendition of Ruth requires a closer look at the primary enigma of the ode: the nightingale. The nightingale is something of a muse who lures the poet into the tender night, awakening his poetic senses in the dark, urging him to feel the "flowers at [his] feet" without seeing them. The nightingale's song leads him to ruminate about the "blushful Hippocrene," the intoxicating spring of the muses at Helicon, analogous to wine, "with beaded bubbles winking at the brim." But on second thought, he prefers to fly toward the bird—not with the chariots of Bacchus, "But on the viewless wings of Poesy."[7]

Though Keats's nightingale seems to be synonymous with the classical muses, she is a darker, Romantic muse whose song has much in common with the Sirens' song on the verge of the abyss. Far from being only a happy, "light-winged" bird among the trees, she is also a strange, nocturnal creature who is associated with the numberless shadows of a summer night, with the dissolving of consciousness, with death. At the very last minute, the speaker realizes that while the bird and her song are destined to be immortal, he cannot escape his humanity. He withdraws abruptly, trying to restore his sense of self and life as he parts from the nightingale.

It is at this dramatic moment of realization that Ruth emerges:

> Thou wast not born for death, immortal Bird!
> No hungry generations tread thee down;
> The voice I hear this passing night was heard
> In ancient days by emperor and clown:
> Perhaps the self-same song that found a path
> Through the sad heart of Ruth, when, sick for home,
> She stood in tears amid the alien corn.

The speaker extols the nightingale for her immortality, for being capable of escaping human sorrow. Her song was not born for death and is not merely the product of that "passing night." It was heard already in ancient times by admirers from all walks of life—be they emperors or clowns. Ruth's song merges with that of the nightingale ("the self-same song"), but not entirely. Unlike the song of the "immortal Bird," it embodies a melancholy, "sad heart" that knows the sorrows of "hungry generations" and is aware of the limits of all human endeavors.

Against the familiar pastoral representations of Ruth gleaning peacefully with a bundle of sheaves in her hands, Keats introduces a sense of alienation and homesickness into this idyllic setting. In the biblical text itself Ruth does not cry in the fields, but she does define herself as a lowly nokhriya, foreigner, in her exchange with Boaz. Keats fills in the lacunae of the biblical tale and imagines what a bereaved migrant gleaner must have felt on searching for sustenance far from home. Keats departs more dramatically from the biblical text in endowing Ruth with a song (there are no songs in the book of Ruth). Keats's Ruth is both the song's ancient listener and its implicit singer much as the speaker of "Ode to a Nightingale" listens to the song whose beauty he captures in his ode. Why Keats chose to cast Ruth in this role is something of a mystery. We can surmise that the ancient gleaner ignites his imagination precisely because she is a songless homesick stranger. She lures him to seek inspiration where it is least expected: in the unheard song of a Moabite woman, whose future, as she gleans in the fields of Bethlehem, is still far from promising. In Ruth, Keats finds something the nightingale lacks: the kind of human resilience to continue gleaning—or singing—even "amid the alien corn."[8]

Keats is not the only artist to have envisioned Ruth as a muse of sorts, though his poem offers the most elaborate rendition of the ancient gleaner in this garb. In some of the readings we followed, we can discern a similar notion. In the Midrash, Ruth is associated with David's singing of the psalms at midnight; in the Zohar she becomes an enchanting tor, a turtledove, who saturates the world above with her singing; in "Kaddish," Ginsberg addresses his mad, Ruth-like mother as a "glorious muse"; and in Song of Solomon, Morrison's most daring Ruth, Pilate (who is also associated with flight), preserves old songs and generates new ones.[9] In more diffuse ways, however, this is also true of all the other afterlives we explored. Ruth, we discover time and again, has found a path into the hearts of many hungry generations, from ancient days until today, inspiring readers, in ever surprising ways, to retell her tale.

It is difficult to part from Ruth, you know. But then, luckily, she never quite leaves us, determined as she is to follow us wherever we go.

NOTES

Introduction

1. The King James Bible's translation of Genesis 30:1.
2. Note that *hesed* has a range of meanings in the Bible: kindness, loving kindness, benevolence, generosity, loyalty, duty, justice.
3. Unless otherwise indicated, biblical citations are from Robert Alter's translation, *The Hebrew Bible* (New York: Norton, 2018).
4. On the interweaving of history and literature in the biblical text, see Robert Alter, *The Art of Biblical Narrative* (New York: Basic, 1981), chap. 2.
5. Martin Buber, *Moses: The Revelation and the Covenant* (Atlantic Highlands, N.J.: Humanities Press International, 1946), 13–19.
6. A female judge is not an unheard-of position. There is one female judge in the book of Judges: Deborah.
7. Toni Morrison, "Goodness: Altruism and the Literary Imagination," a talk delivered at Harvard Divinity School, De-

cember 2012, https://www.nytimes.com/2019/08/07/books/toni
-morrison-goodness-altruism-literary-imagination.html.

8. For an extended survey of the different scholarly datings
of the book of Ruth, see the new Anchor Yale Bible commentary
on Ruth by Jeremy Schipper (New Haven: Yale University Press,
2016), 18–22.

9. See S. D. Goitein's discussion of Ruth's female author in
Studies in the Bible (Tel Aviv: Yavneh, 1963), 252 (in Hebrew), and
Edward F. Campbell, *Ruth: A New Translation with Introduction and
Commentary*, Anchor Yale Bible (New Haven: Yale University Press,
1975), 23.

10. See Fokkelien Van-Dijk Hemmes, "Ruth: A Product of
Women's Cultures?" in Athalya Brenner's *A Feminist Companion to
Ruth* (Sheffield, U.K.: Sheffield Academic Press, 1993), 134–144.

11. Walter Benjamin, "The Task of the Translator," in *Illuminations*, trans. Harry Zohn (New York: Schocken, 1955), 73.

Chapter 1. The Moabite

1. In biblical law, the stranger, the orphan, and the widow—
ha-ger, ha-yatom ve-ha'almanah—often appear together as representatives of the underprivileged who deserve special care. We shall
consider this legal category (primarily in discussing the law regu-
lating gleaning) in the next section.

2. The word *re'uta*, "her female friend," appears in Exodus
11:2 and Esther 1:19.

3. For a consideration of the poetic insets in the book of
Ruth, see Robert Alter's introduction to the book in *The Hebrew
Bible* III, 623–624.

4. See Bonnie Honig, "Ruth, the Model Emigrée: Mourn-
ing and the Symbolic Politics of Immigration," *Political Theory* 25,
no. 1 (1997): 112–136.

5. Alter, *The Art of Biblical Narrative*, 129. Alter provides extensive consideration of the art of the biblical conception of character; see in particular chapters 6 and 8. The first to call attention
to the lacunae in the portrayal of biblical characters was the literary
critic Erich Auerbach. See Auerbach's *Mimesis: The Representation*

of Reality in Western Literature, trans. Willard R. Trask (1953; Princeton: Princeton University Press, 2003), chap. 1.

6. For readings of Naomi's silence as stemming from her ambivalence vis-à-vis Ruth's Moabite origin, see Avivah Zornberg, "The Concealed Alternative," in *Reading Ruth: Contemporary Women Reclaim a Sacred Story*, ed. Judith A. Kates and Gail Twersky Reimer (New York: Ballantine, 1994), 65–82; Honig, "Ruth, the Model Emigrée."

7. For more on the ways in which Ruth and Naomi share their respective migrations, see Ilana Pardes, *Countertraditions in the Bible: A Feminist Approach* (Cambridge: Harvard University Press, 1992), 112–115.

8. On Ruth and Job, see Yair Zakovitch, *Ruth* (Jerusalem: Magnes and Am Oved, 1990), 30–31 (in Hebrew). The closest Joban verse to Naomi's cry is Job 27:2: "By God, Who denied me justice / and by Shaddai Who embittered my life."

9. Julia Kristeva, *Strangers to Ourselves*, trans. Leon S. Roudiez (New York: Columbia University Press, 1991), 17–18.

10. Human rights are a modern concept, conceived primarily within the context of the Enlightenment, but the law of gleaning serves as one of the precursors for this legal category. See Haim H. Cohen, *Human Rights in the Bible and Talmud* (Woodstock, Vt.: Jewish Lights, 1997). For more on the biblical welfare system and the law of gleaning, see Benjamin Porat, *The Principles of Welfare Regulations: From Biblical Law to Rabbinic Literature* (Jerusalem: Sacher Institute & IDI, 2019) (in Hebrew).

11. See also Leviticus 19:9–10. "And when you reap your land's harvest you shall not finish off the edge of your field, nor pick up the gleanings of your harvest. . . . For the poor and for the sojourner you shall leave them."

12. The meaning of the name "Boaz" is uncertain. In later rabbinic commentaries it is perceived as symbolic, associated with the Hebrew term for strength: *oz*.

13. Robert Alter traces a modification of the betrothal typescene in this episode in *The Art of Biblical Narrative*, 58.

14. For more on the biblical distinction between *ger* and *nokhri*,

see Ishay Rosen-Zvi and Adi Ophir, *Goy: Israel's Multiple Others and the Birth of the Gentile* (Oxford: Oxford University Press, 2018), chap. 1. The figurative sense of *nokhri* is apparent in Job 19:15— "Those who dwelled in my house and my slavegirls / reckoned me as a stranger (*nokhri*)."

15. For more on the book of Ruth and the story of Sodom, see Tikva Frymer-Kensky, *Reading the Women of the Bible: A New Interpretation of Their Stories* (New York: Schocken, 2002), 258–263. On the story of Sodom and the question of sexuality, see Ronald Hendel, Chana Kronfeld, and Ilana Pardes, "Gender and Sexuality," in *Reading Genesis: Ten Methods*, ed. Ronald Hendel (Cambridge: Cambridge University Press, 2010), 71–91.

16. The term *lie* appears throughout the scene and has distinct sexual connotations in biblical Hebrew. Note that it also appears in 3:13–14. In addition to the ambiguities of lie the use of the verb *yada*, "know," in this chapter is also endowed with sexual undertones.

17. It is noteworthy that Ruth's uncovering of Boaz's feet calls to mind the biblical expression for incest in biblical law: "to lay bare nakedness" (Leviticus 18).

18. On Ruth's boldness in this scene, see Phyllis Trible, *God and the Rhetoric of Sexuality* (Philadelphia: Fortress, 1978), 181–187.

19. This is a slightly modified version of Robert Alter's translation. The term *kanaf* means both "wing" and the "corner of a garment." Alter chooses "skirt" in translating Ezekiel 16:8 and "wing" in his translation of Ruth 3:9.

20. A slightly modified version of Robert Alter's translation. On Boaz's unexpected presentation of Ruth's hesed in this exchange, see Mieke Bal, *Lethal Love: Feminist Literary Readings of Biblical Love Stories* (Bloomington: Indiana University Press, 1987), 72–87.

21. It is no coincidence that a humiliating legal procedure awaits those who refuse to implement the levirate law as is indicated in Deuteronomy 25:9.

22. For more on the merging of the law of redemption and the levirate law in the book of Ruth, see Daniel Friedman, *To Kill*

and Inherit (Tel Aviv: Dvir, 2000), chaps. 16 and 17 (in Hebrew); Adele Berlin, "Legal Fiction: Levirate *cum* Land Redemption in Ruth," *Journal of Ancient Judaism* 1 (2010): 3–18.

23. The respective stories of migration in Genesis 31 and the book of Ruth are also interconnected. Feeling like strangers in their father's house, Rachel and Leah are eager to move to Canaan in search of a better life. In doing so, they anticipate Naomi's sense of self estrangement and above all Ruth's bold decision to leave her family and homeland and head to an unknown land. For an extensive consideration of the book of Ruth as a revision of the story of Rachel and Leah, see Pardes, *Countertraditions in the Bible*, chap. 6.

24. A slightly modified version of Alter's translation.

25. The name Mahlon is associated with illness in the book of Ruth, but etymologically speaking, it may be akin to "sweetness." In fact, the name Mahlon may be related to other biblical names, primarily Mahla (Numbers 26:33) or Mahli (Exodus 6:19). For a consideration of various scholarly accounts of the names Mahlon and Chilion, see Schipper, *Ruth*, 82.

Chapter 2. The Convert

1. On the invention of the gentile in rabbinic culture, see Adi Ophir and Ishay Rosen-Zvi, *Goy: Israel's Multiple Others and the Birth of the Gentile* (Oxford: Oxford University Press, 2018), 179–185.

2. Ephraim Urbach provides a helpful contextualization of the rise of Jewish conversion in Late Antiquity. See Ephraim E. Urbach, *The Sages: Their Concepts and Beliefs*, trans. Israel Abrahams (Jerusalem: Magnes, 1975), 541–554.

3. Mekhilta d'Rabbi Yishmael, Mishpatim, quoted in Urbach, *The Sages*, 549.

4. Midrash Tanhuma-Yelammedenu, *lekh lekha* 6, in *Midrash Tanhuma-Yelammedenu: An English Translation of Genesis and Exodus from the Printed Version of Tanhuma-Yelammedenu*, ed. and trans. Samuel A. Berman (Hoboken, N.J.: KTAV Publishing House, 1996), 88.

5. Babylonian Talmud (hereafter "BT"), Yevamot 47b, quoted in Urbach, *The Sages*, 550.

6. BT, Shabbat 31a (translation mine).

7. Ecclesiastes Rabbah, 5:11, 1, quoted in Urbach, *The Sages*, 553.

8. *Rabba* means "great," attesting to the sizable volume of Ruth Rabbah. The smaller, later corpus of midrashim on the book of Ruth is Ruth Zuta.

9. The main sources of Ruth Rabbah are the Jerusalem Talmud, Bereshit Rabbah, Vayikra Rabbah, and Eichah Rabbah.

10. Galit Hasan-Rokem, *Tales of the Neighborhood: Jewish Narrative Dialogues in Late Antiquity* (Berkeley: University of California Press, 2003). For a literary-psychoanalytic consideration of the tensions between the worlds of the house of study and the familial sphere, see Haim Weiss and Shira Stav, *The Return of the Missing Father: New Perspectives on a Series of Stories from the Babylonian Talmud* (Jerusalem: Mosad Bialik, 2018) (in Hebrew).

11. Eglon King of Moab oppressed the Israelites until Ehud ben Gera (one of the judges) killed him by sword (Judges 3:14–30).

12. All translations of Ruth Rabbah are mine; the biblical citations within these quotations are from Robert Alter's translation: *The Hebrew Bible* (New York: Norton, 2018).

13. See also Sanhedrin 107:2.

14. See Shaye J. D. Cohen, *The Beginning of Jewishness: Boundaries, Varieties, Uncertainties* (Berkeley: University of California Press, 1999), 218–219, 232–233.

15. William James, *The Varieties of Religious Experience* (New York: Collier, 1961), 160.

16. Quoted in Cohen, *The Beginning of Jewishness*, 199–200.

17. For more on the Talmud's understanding of the convert's admission test, see Cohen, *The Beginning of Jewishness*, chap. 7.

18. On the question of Ruth's modesty, see Maren Niehoff, "Constructing Ruth's Image in the Midrash," *Jerusalem Studies in Jewish Thought* 11 (1993): 49–78 (in Hebrew), and Tamar Meir, *A Moabite Girl: Halakhah and the Process of Acceptance in Midrash Ruth Rabbah* (Tel Aviv: Resling, 2019) (in Hebrew), 52–64.

19. Daniel Boyarin, *Intertextuality and the Reading of Midrash* (Bloomington: Indiana University Press, 1990).

20. James Kugel looks at the rabbinic fascination with the irregularities of the biblical text in "Two Introductions to Midrash," in *Midrash and Literature*, ed. Geoffrey Hartman and Sanford Budick (New Haven: Yale University Press, 1986), 92–93.

21. On the folkloric bent of the Midrash, see Galit Hasan-Rokem, *Web of Life: Folklore and Midrash in Rabbinic Literature* (Stanford: Stanford University Press, 2000).

22. For a consideration of the question of purity in the construction of Jewish identities, see Christine E. Hayes, *Gentile Impurities and Jewish Identities: Intermarriage and Conversion from the Bible to the Talmud* (Oxford: Oxford University Press, 2002). On menstruation in rabbinic culture, see Charlotte Elisheva Fonrobert, *Menstrual Purity: Rabbinic and Christian Reconstructions of Biblical Gender* (Stanford: Stanford University Press, 2000); Shai Secunda, *The Talmud's Red Fence: Menstrual Impurity and Difference in Babylonian Judaism and Its Sasanian Context* (Oxford: Oxford University Press, 2020).

23. See BT, Tractate Kiddushin 1:1.

24. If the change is not a scribal error, Ruth may be referring to Boaz's generous suggestion that she approach the young men should she be thirsty and ask them to draw water for her.

25. See Niehoff, "Constructing Ruth's Image in the Midrash," for a consideration of unflattering commentaries on Ruth's lewdness both in Ruth Rabbah and in Ruth Zuta.

26. In Ruth Zuta (1:1), Ruth is designated as *'ima shel malkhut*, the "mother of royalty." Although this designation does not appear in Ruth Rabbah, it is wholly compatible with the representation of Ruth in this midrashic corpus as well.

27. BT, Tractate Berakhot 7b.

28. In positioning Bathsheba on the throne of the king's mother, this commentary follows the description in 1 Kings 2:19.

29. For more on Solomon's judgment, see Steven Weitzman, *Solomon: The Lure of Wisdom* (New Haven: Yale University Press, 2011), chap. 4.

30. See Isaiah 11:1. On the beginnings of messianism in the Bible, see Yair Zakovitch, "'A Lowly Man Riding on an Ass' (Zechariah 9:9)," in *The Messianic Idea in Jewish Thought* (Jerusalem: Israel Academy of Sciences and Humanities, 1982), 7–17 (in Hebrew).

31. For more on the messianic dimension of the midrashic adaptations of Ruth's tale, see Charlotte Elisheva Fonrobert, "The Handmaid, the Trickster and the Birth of the Messiah," in *Current Trends in the Study of Midrash*, ed. Carol Bakhos (Leiden: Brill, 2006), 245–275. For a broader consideration of the rabbinic perspectives on the Messiah, see Hasan-Rokem, *Web of Life*, chap. 8.

32. There are several patristic commentaries on the book of Ruth, but most of them are brief. Among the patristic exegetes who commented on Ruth are: Ephrem the Syrian, Ambrose of Milan, and Jerome. For more on Ephrem's commentary on Ruth, see Jane Richardson Jensen, "Ruth According to Ephrem the Syrian," in *A Feminist Companion to the Book of Ruth*, ed. Athalya Brenner (Sheffield, U.K.: Sheffield Academic Press, 2001), 170–176. For an overview of early Christian exegesis on the book of Ruth, see John R. Franke, ed., *Joshua, Judges, Ruth, 1–2 Samuel: Ancient Christian Commentary on Scripture* (Downers Grove, Ill.: InterVarsity Press, 2005), 181–192. The paucity of commentaries on the book of Ruth is striking when compared to the profusion of Christian exegesis on the Song of Songs. For more on Christian commentaries on the Song of Songs in Late Antiquity, see Ilana Pardes, *The Song of Songs: A Biography* (Princeton: Princeton University Press, 2019), chap. 1.

33. Quotation from the King James Version.

34. On the interrelations of the Jewish and Christian configurations of the birth of the Messiah, see Ruth Kara-Ivanov Kaniel, *Holiness and Transgression: Mothers of the Messiah in the Jewish Myth*, trans. Eugene D. Matansky with Ruth Kara-Ivanov Kaniel (Boston: Academic Studies Press, 2017), 219–252.

35. My translation. Tobiah ben Eliezer was a Bulgarian Talmudist and a poet. *Lekach Tov* is a midrashic commentary on the Pentateuch and the Five Scrolls, among them the book of Ruth.

36. Simhah ben Samuel of Vitry was a pupil of Rashi who lived

in Vitry-le-François. *Machzor Vitry* contains decisions and rules concerning religious practice, besides responsa by Rashi and other authorities, both contemporary and earlier.

Chapter 3. The Shekhinah in Exile

1. BT, Megilla 29a (translation mine).

2. For more on the Shekhinah, see Gershom Scholem, *Major Trends in Jewish Mysticism* (New York: Schocken, 1961); Ephraim E. Urbach, *The Sages: Their Concepts and Beliefs* (Jerusalem: Magnes, 1975), 37–65; Moshe Idel, *Kabbalah and Eros* (New Haven: Yale University Press, 2005).

3. Other notable biblical women associated with the Shekhinah include Rachel, Tamar, Miriam, Esther, and the beloved of the Song of Songs.

4. See Arthur Green, "Shekhinah, the Virgin Mary, and the Song of Songs," *AJS Review* 26, no. 1 (2002): 1–44. Green's article generated a heated debate among scholars of Kabbalah. Yehuda Liebes refutes the possibility that Marian worship could have had any impact on configurations of the Shekhinah, one of his major points being the pronounced difference between the virginity of Mary and the overt sexuality of the Shekhinah. To be sure, there are important distinctions between the Shekhinah and Mary, but influence, especially in polemical contexts, cannot but be partial. For more on the Shekhinah and Mary, see Peter Schaefer, *Mirror of Her Beauty: Feminine Images of God from the Bible to Early Kabbalah* (Princeton: Princeton University Press, 2002).

5. In shaping the image of the exilic Shekhinah, the Kabbalists may have been influenced in particular by the configurations of Mary as the sorrowful mother mourning the crucifixion of her son. Interestingly, the well-known hymn *Stabat Mater Dolorosa* was composed around the same time, in the thirteenth century. For more on the Shekhinah and the *Stabat Mater,* see Haviva Pedaya, "A Genealogy of the Shekhinah and the Mother," in *As a Perennial Spring: A Festschrift Honoring Rabbi Dr. Norman,* ed. Bentsi Cohen (New York: Lamm, 2013), 87–151 (in Hebrew).

6. For an overview of the history of the composition of the

Zohar and the Spanish context, see Arthur Green's introduction to *The Zohar*, ed. and trans. Daniel C. Matt, 12 vols., Pritzker Edition (Stanford: Stanford University Press, 2004–2017), 1:xxxi–lxxxi. All quotations from the Zohar are from this edition.

7. *Midrash Ha-Ne'lam* is a collection of commentaries that were omitted from the earliest printed Zohar editions but were later culled from manuscript sources. The dating of *Midrash Ha-Ne'lam* has been disputed. Although most scholars regard this corpus as earlier than the main body of the Zohar (*guf ha-Zohar*), some consider it a later source. Either way, its date of composition is close to that of the main body of the Zohar.

8. The portion of *Midrash Ha-Ne'lam* devoted to Ruth's tale is also called *Zohar Ruth* or *Zohar Hadash Ruth*.

9. ZH 79a, *Zohar*, 11:104–105 (trans. Joel Hecker). (Daniel Matt is general editor of the Pritzker edition and translated volumes 1–10. Joel Hecker translated volume 11.)

10. ZH 78b, *Zohar*, 11:92 (trans. Hecker).

11. Another hidden drama takes place behind the scenes. Both Ruth and Boaz belong to a world of *sefirot*, divine emanations. Ruth is associated with the *sefira* of the Shekhinah, "Kingdom" (*malkhut*), and Boaz is primarily linked to the *sefira* of the blessed Holy One "Beauty" (*tif'eret*) and occasionally to "Foundation" (*yesod*). Any negotiation between Ruth and Boaz has an impact on the entire supernal tree of the sefirot. For an extensive account of the sefirot and their interrelations, see Green's introduction, *Zohar*, 1:xlv–liii.

12. Translation of Ruth 3:8 from Robert Alter, *The Hebrew Bible* (New York: Norton, 2018).

13. ZH 88b, *Zohar*, 11:237 (trans. Hecker).

14. For more on the exilic Ruth-like Shekhinah in *Midrash Ha-Ne'lam*, see Ruth Kara-Ivanov Kaniel, *Holiness and Transgression: Mothers of the Messiah in the Jewish Myth*, trans. Eugene D. Matansky with Ruth Kara-Ivanov Kaniel (Boston: Academic Studies Press, 2017), 188–201.

15. Ruth in this Zoharic rendition blends with Jeremiah's Ra-

chel, who cries over her exiled children, refusing to be consoled (Jeremiah 31:14).

16. Pedaya, "A Genealogy of the Shekhinah and the Mother," 104–106. Pedaya is inspired by the rabbinic tradition according to which the Messiah was born on Tisha B'av, on the day of the destruction of the Temple. The midrashic justification for this peculiar birthdate is that the ultimate agony is not devoid of an element of hope.

17. ZH 88b, *Zohar*, 11:239 (trans. Hecker).

18. See Gershom Scholem, *The Messianic Idea in Judaism and Other Essays on Jewish Spirituality* (New York: Schocken, 1971); Stéphane Mosès, *The Angel of History: Rosenzweig, Benjamin, Scholem*, trans. Barbara Harshav (Stanford: Stanford University Press, 2009), 129–144; David Biale, *Gershom Scholem: Master of the Kabbalah* (New Haven: Yale University Press, 2018).

19. Franz Kafka, *Parables and Paradoxes*, ed. Nahum N. Glatzer (New York: Schocken, 1961), 81.

20. ZH 88b, *Zohar*, 11:237 (trans. Hecker).

21. The connection between Ruth and David makes more sense in Zoharic eyes given that both are associated with the sefira of the Shekhinah. David is the only male biblical character who is associated with the Shekhinah. His connection to a feminine Shekhinah is not as surprising as it may seem given that this sefira is designated as Malkhut, Kingdom. The textual clue the Zohar's authors rely on is the word *bahurim*, "young men," in Ruth 3:10. It reminds them of the name of the town from which Shimei emerges to curse David, Bahurim (2 Samuel 16:5).

22. ZH 88b, *Zohar*, 11:238 (trans. Hecker).

23. Gershom Scholem, "Redemption Through Sin," in *The Messianic Idea in Judaism*, 78–141.

24. Scholem regarded the catastrophe of the expulsion from Spain as the major incentive for the rise of messianism, but later generations of Kabbalah scholars traced the beginnings of mystical messianic configurations in the Zohar. See Moshe Idel, *Messianic Mystics* (New Haven: Yale University Press, 1988); Yehuda

Liebes, *Studies in Jewish Myth and Jewish Messianism*, trans. Batya Stein (Albany: State University of New York Press, 1993); Haviva Pedaya, *Vision and Speech: Models of Prophecy in Jewish Mysticism* (Los Angeles: Kruv, 2002).

25. It is noteworthy that the centrality of sexuality in the Zohar is not limited to messianic phenomena. For more on the different Zoharic perspectives on eros, see Moshe Idel, *Kabbalah and Eros*; Yehuda Liebes, "Zohar and Eros," *Alpayim* 9 (1994): 67–119 (in Hebrew); Elliot R. Wolfson, *Language, Eros, Being: Kabbalistic Hermeneutics and Poetic Imagination* (New York: Fordham University Press, 2005); Melila Hellner-Eshed, *A River Flows from Eden: The Language of Mystical Experience in the Zohar*, trans. Nathan Wolski (Stanford: Stanford University Press, 2009).

26. Zohar 1:110b–111a, *Zohar*, 2:159–161 (trans. Matt).

27. See Matt's note on this intricate Kabbalistic wordplay in *Zohar*, 2:160 (trans. Matt).

28. Zohar 1:110b–111a, *Zohar*, 2:160 (trans. Matt).

29. See Kara-Ivanov Kaniel, *Holiness and Transgression*, 124–145.

30. Tamar, like Ruth, is both a woman and a Shekhinah in the Zohar, which is why the merging of these two women is even more understandable.

31. Zohar 1:188b, *Zohar*, 3:149–150 (trans. Matt).

32. It is noteworthy that levirate marriage in the Zohar is a mode of reincarnation. The dead actually come back to life through their offspring. In implementing the levirate law, Tamar and Ruth both preserve the names of their deceased husbands and enhance their reincarnation. For more on the Zohar's perception of levirate marriage, see Gershom Scholem, *On the Mystical Shape of the Godhead: Basic Concepts in the Kabbalah*, trans. Joachim Neugroschel, ed. and rev. Jonathan Chipman (New York: Schocken, 1991), 197–250.

33. See Matt's note on this verb in *Zohar*, 3:149 (trans. Matt). For more on the recurrent use of the verb *ishtaddalat* in this passage and the interrelations of Ruth and Tamar, see Kara-Ivanov Kaniel, *Holiness and Transgression*, 183–188.

34. The companions have double lives at night: while engag-

ing in Torah study in this world, their souls ascend to the Garden of Eden to take part in celestial exegetical delights with the blessed Holy One.

35. Note that the obligation to meditate on the Torah "day and night" appears in Joshua 1:8. It is one of God's primary demands in the book of Joshua. Whereas in the biblical text the expression is meant to convey the importance of total devotion to God's decrees, in the Zoharic world it is regarded as a call to literally meditate on the Torah day and night.

36. Hellner-Eshed, *A River Flows from Eden*, 125.

37. In *Midrash Ha-Ne'lam* we find an explicit association of the threshing floor scene with the nocturnal study of the righteous— see ZH 88a, *Zohar*, 11:234 (trans. Hecker).

38. ZH 86a, *Zohar*, 11:205 (trans. Hecker). To be more precise, the Shekhinah and Ruth are associated with the Oral Torah, with the later commentaries that were added to the Written Torah. But since according to the Midrash, the Oral Torah and the Written Torah were given simultaneously at Sinai, the Ruth-like Shekhinah is linked to Scripture as a whole.

39. ZH 85b, *Zohar*, 11:196 (trans. Hecker).

40. On the Midrash's approach to the Song of Songs, see Daniel Boyarin, *Intertextuality and the Reading of Midrash* (Bloomington: Indiana University Press, 1990); Pardes, *The Song of Songs: A Biography* (Princeton: Princeton University Press, 2019), chap. 1.

41. On the fallen, sorrowful Shekhinah of *Tikkunei Zohar*, see Biti Roi, *The Love of the Shekhinah: Mysticism and Poetics in Tikkunei Zohar* (Ramat Gan: Bar-Ilan University Press, 2016) (in Hebrew).

42. *Tikkunei Zohar* 31:75b–76a (translation mine).

43. Zohar 1:8a, *Zohar*, 1:51–52 (trans. Matt).

44. The first record of the ritual appears in a letter by Shlomo Alkabetz (c. 1505–1584) that offers an account of Joseph Karo and his followers performing a Tikkun Leil Shavuot in what is in all likelihood Nicopolis.

45. Reading passages from *Midrash Ha-Ne'lam* on Ruth may have been part of the ritual of Shavuot before the invention of Tikkun Leil Shavuot. There are approximately one hundred man-

uscripts of the section of *Midrash Ha-Ne'lam* devoted to the book of Ruth, mostly dating from the fourteenth and fifteenth centuries. This is an exceptionally high number of manuscripts (no other Zoharic text has such a record). We have no information regarding their use, but the profusion of remaining manuscripts may be seen as evidence that the Zoharic corpus on Ruth was part of the liturgy of Shavuot for several centuries. For more on these manuscripts, see Daniel Abrams's introduction to *Midrash Ha-Ne'lam Ruth*, Facsimile Edition of Venice 1566 (Jerusalem: self-published, 1992) (in Hebrew); Yonatan Benarroch, "Yanuka and Sava—Two That Are One: Allegory, Symbol and Myth in Zoharic Literature" (Ph.D. diss., Hebrew University of Jerusalem, 2012), 263–270.

Chapter 4. The Pastoral Gleaner

1. For more on the history of the pastoral, see Frank Kermode, *English Pastoral Poetry: From the Beginnings to Marvell* (London: Harrap, 1952); Peter V. Marinelli, *Pastoral* (London: Methuen, 1971); Terry Gifford, *Pastoral* (London: Routledge, 1999).

2. Theocritus, idyll 7, trans. C. S. Calverley, https://www.gutenberg.org/files/11533/11533-h/11533-h.htm. For more on the pastoral otium, see Thomas G. Rosenmeyer, *The Green Cabinet: Theocritus and the European Pastoral Lyric* (Berkeley: University of California Press, 1973).

3. Paul Alpers addresses the question of the representation of social realities in Virgil's *Eclogues* in *What Is Pastoral?* (Chicago: Chicago University Press, 1996).

4. On the return of the pastoral in Renaissance literature, see Kermode, *English Pastoral Poetry*, 32–44. For more on the pastoral in Renaissance art, see Luba Freedman, *The Classical Pastoral in the Visual Arts* (New York: Peter Lang, 1989).

5. The Octateuch includes the first eight books of the Bible. In the Greek and Latin Bibles, the book of Ruth follows the book of Judges (as is the case in the King James Bible) and so is the eighth book. For an extensive consideration of medieval iconography of Ruth, see Sarit Shalev-Eyni, "In the Days of the Barley Har-

vest: The Iconography of Ruth," *Atibus et Historiae* 26, no. 51 (2005): 37–57. Shalev-Eyni also provides a consideration of the interrelations between Jewish and Christian illuminations in diverse medieval contexts. For more on Bibles moralisées, see John Lowden, *The Making of the Bibles Moralisées* (University Park: Pennsylvania State University Press, 2000), 1–9, 199–209; Martin O'Kane, "The Iconography of the Book of Ruth," *Interpretation* 64, no. 2 (April 2010): 130–145.

6. See John R. Franke, ed., *Joshua, Judges, Ruth, 1–2 Samuel: Ancient Christian Commentary on Scripture* (Downers Grove, Ill.: InterVarsity Press, 2005), 181–192.

7. Cited in Richard Verdi, *Poussin as Painter: From Classicism to Abstraction* (London: Reaktion, 2020), 297.

8. Much has been written on Poussin's landscapes. See in particular Anthony Blunt, "The Heroic and the Ideal Landscapes in the Work of Nicolas Poussin," *Journal of the Warburg and Courtauld Institutes* 7 (1944): 154–168; Alain Mérot, "The Conquest of Space: Poussin's Early Attempts at Landscape," in *Poussin and Nature: Arcadian Visions*, ed. Pierre Rosenberg and Keith Christiansen (New York: Met Publications, 2007), 51–71.

9. See Willibald Sauerländer, "'Nature Through the Glass of Time': A Reflection on the Meaning of Poussin's Landscapes," in *Poussin and Nature*, 103–117.

10. Poussin sets Ruth as Eve's opposite. Eve is rendered in *Spring* as a beautiful, seductive, and naked woman.

11. On Poussin's *Summer* as resembling an annunciation scene, see Alain Mérot, *Nicolas Poussin* (New York: Abbeville, 1990), 249. It is noteworthy that another Christian symbol hovers in the background of this painting—that of the Eucharist (both bread and wine are present). It becomes more apparent when we consider the wine that is celebrated in *Autumn*. See Anthony Blunt's discussion of the echoes of the Eucharist in "The Last Synthesis: *The Four Seasons* and the *Apollo and Daphne*," in Blunt, *Nicolas Poussin* (London: Pallas Athene, 1967), 332–356.

12. There are various renditions of the myth of Demeter and

Persephone. I follow the Homeric hymn "To Demeter." See *The Homeric Hymns*, trans. Apostolos N. Athanassakis (Baltimore: Johns Hopkins University Press, 1976), 1–15.

13. For more on Poussin's *Et in Arcadia Ego*, see Erwin Panofsky, "'Et in Arcadia Ego': Poussin and the Elegiac Tradition," in *Philosophy and History: Essays Presented to Ernst Cassirer*, ed. R. Klibansky and H. J. Paton (Oxford: Clarendon, 1936), 257–262; Freedman, *The Classical Pastoral in the Visual Arts*, 115–126.

14. Koch's painting is at the Milwaukee Art Museum and can be seen at a number of online sites, including https://www.bing.com/images/search?view=detailV2&ccid=Xidbojp9&id=C5DEF3A69 737761136A8D42047FB2948E1583C4F&thid=OIP.Xidbojp949 EruMoH_jTJ2QHaFu&mediaurl=https%3a%2f%2flh6.ggpht.com %2fUQ96glqjXoqdhuRFvHiT3OncSdRA.

15. Jonathan Sheehan, *The Enlightenment Bible: Translation, Scholarship, Culture* (Princeton: Princeton University Press, 2005), front flap and ix; Renan's *Vie de Jésus* was a French response to its German precursor: David Friedrich Strauss's *The Life of Jesus* (1835–1836).

16. For more on Millet's life and work, see Griselda Pollock, *Millet* (London: Oresko, 1977); Alexandra Murphy, *Jean-François Millet* (Boston: Museum of Fine Arts, Boston, 1984).

17. In a sense, Millet foregrounds what is only marginal in the Virgilian pastoral: the confiscations of land and scarcity that are only too prevalent in the rural world.

18. See Liana Vardi, "Construing the Harvest: Gleaners, Farmers, and Officials in Early Modern France," *American Historical Review* 98, no. 5 (December 1993): 1424–1447, specifically 1437–1439.

19. The right to glean did not apply to destitute foreigners in Europe because immigrants were not a major social factor up until the twentieth century.

20. See Vardi, "Construing the Harvest," 1439–1447.

21. For more on Millet's *Gleaners*, see Bradley Fratello, "The Intertwined Fates of 'The Gleaners' and 'The Angelus,'" *Art Bulletin* 85, no. 4 (December 2003): 685–701.

22. Quoted in Fratello, "The Intertwined Fates of 'The Gleaners' and 'The Angelus,'" 687.

23. See Pollock, *Millet*, 17. The full citation, by the critic Paul de Saint Victor, goes as follows: "His three gleaners have gigantic pretensions, they pose as the Three Fates of Poverty . . . their ugliness and their grossness unrelieved."

24. Quoted in Hans W. Frei, *The Eclipse of Biblical Narrative: A Study in Eighteenth and Nineteenth Century Hermeneutics* (New Haven: Yale University Press, 1974), 185.

25. Elsewhere, in his commentary and translation of the Song of Songs, Herder provides a detailed account of the affinity between biblical poetry and the pastoral heritage of the East. For more on Herder's reading of the Song of Songs as a product of oriental imagination, see Pardes, *The Song of Songs: A Biography*, 136–147.

26. J. W. Goethe, *West-Eastern Divan*, trans. Martin Bidney and Peter Anton von Arnim (New York: State University of New York Press, 2010), 177.

27. For more on nineteenth-century Holy Land travel narratives, see Hilton Obenzinger, *American Palestine: Melville, Twain, and the Holy Land Mania* (Princeton: Princeton University Press, 1999). Obenzinger focuses on the American scene but provides background regarding the development of the genre in the European context as well.

28. Not much has been written on Merle. For a brief consideration of his work, see Eitner Lorenz, *French Painting of the Nineteenth Century*, Part I: *Before Impressionism* (Washington, D.C.: National Gallery of Art, Distributed by Oxford University Press, 2000), 310–312. A succinct biography is provided by Rehs Galleries: https://rehs.com/eng/default-19th20th-century-artist-bio-page /?fl_builder&artist_no=731&sold=1. In 1879 at least fifty-two works by Merle were in private hands of American collectors: see Edward Strahan, *The Art Treasures of America; Being the Choicest Works of Art in the Public and Private Collections of North America* (Philadelphia, 1879), index; see also "Foreign Correspondence, Items, etc.," *The Crayon* 7, no. 10 (October 1, 1860): 296.

29. Another notable French orientalist painter who rendered

Ruth as a sensuous-modest pastoral gleaner was Louis Devedeux. His portrait of Ruth appeared as an illustration in Harriet Beecher Stowe's *Women in Sacred History: A Celebration of Women in the Bible* (1873), one of the most notable nineteenth-century American women's Bibles (sales exceeded fifteen thousand). (The image can be viewed at Wikimedia Commons: https://commons.wikimedia .org/wiki/File:Louis_Devedeux_-_Ruth.jpg.) For an even more seductive oriental Ruth, whose breasts are exposed, see the rendition of 1835 by the Italian artist Francesco Hayez (available at WikiArt: https://www.wikiart.org/en/francesco-hayez/ruth-1835). It is noteworthy that Victor Hugo's renowned poem "Boaz Asleep" ("Booz endormi," 1859) also offers a memorable dreamy blend of sensuousness and chastity.

30. Edward W. Said, *Orientalism* (New York: Vintage, 1978). Said provides a pertinent account regarding orientalism in French literature, from Chateaubriand to Flaubert, in chapter 5, pages 166–197. For more on orientalist art, see Linda Nochlin, "The Imaginary Orient," in Nochlin, *The Politics of Vision: Essays on Nineteenth-Century Art and Society* (New York: Harper & Row, 1989), 33–59.

31. The series consists of 139 plates depicting scenes from the Hebrew Bible, 21 from the Apocrypha, and 81 from the New Testament. For more on Doré's life, see Blanche Roosevelt, *Life and Reminiscence of Gustave Doré* (New York: Cassell, 1885). For a consideration of his biblical illustrations and their influence, see Eric Zafran, ed., *Fantasy and Faith: The Art of Gustave Doré* (New Haven: Yale University Press, 2007), and Sarah C. Schaefer, "'From the Smallest Fragment': The Archaeology of the Doré Bible," *Nineteenth-Century Art Worldwide* 13, no. 1 (Spring 2014), available at http://www.19thc-artworldwide.org/spring14/schaefer-on-the -archaeology-of-the-dore-bible (accessed October 7, 2020).

32. Quoted in Schaefer's "'From the Smallest Fragment,'" 1.

Chapter 5. The Zionist Pioneer

1. For more on the Israeli Bible, see Anita Shapira, "The Bible and Israeli Identity," *AJS Review* 28, no. 1 (2004): 11–42.

2. The letter, "The Bible Shines in Its Own Light," is re-

printed in Ben-Gurion's *Bible Studies* (Tel Aviv: Am Oved, 1969), 41–49 (in Hebrew).

3. Ibid., 48.

4. Other privileged biblical books in Zionist culture are Exodus, Joshua, Samuel, and the Song of Songs. For an account of the book of Joshua in Israeli culture, see Rachel Havrelock, *River Jordan: The Mythology of a Dividing Line* (Chicago: University of Chicago Press, 2011). For an extensive consideration of the Israeli Song of Songs, see Ilana Pardes, *Agnon's Moonstruck Lovers: The Song of Songs in Israeli Culture* (Seattle: University of Washington Press, 2013).

5. For more on Lilien's Bible, see Richard I. Cohen, "Urban Visibility and Biblical Visions: Jewish Culture in Western and Central Europe in the Modern Age," in *Cultures of the Jews*, ed. David Biale (New York: Schocken, 2002), 781–783. See also Richard I. Cohen, *Jewish Icons: Art and Society in Modern Europe* (Berkeley: University of California Press, 1998).

6. Lilien's Ruth is also something of an Abraham. Note the similarities between Lilien's illustration of Ruth and his rendition of the scene in which Abraham steps into the night and is called upon to view the promise that is embedded in the endless stars above. Viewable on Wikimedia Commons, at https://commons.wikimedia.org/wiki/File:Abraham_Lilien.jpg.

7. On women pioneers in early Zionism, see Billie Melman, "From the Margins to the History of the Yishuv: Gender in the Land of Israel, 1890–1920," *Riv'on le-heker toldot Yisrael* (1997): 243–278 (in Hebrew).

8. Quoted in Paul Mendes-Flohr, *Martin Buber: A Life of Faith and Dissent* (New Haven: Yale University Press, 2019), 36. For more on Buber's response to Lilien's art, see pages 35–38.

9. On the unique features of Jewish orientalism, see Ariel Hirschfeld, "Locus and Language: Hebrew Culture in Israel 1890–1990s," in *Cultures of the Jews*, 1011–1060.

10. To be more precise, women in Arab villages usually carry heavy jars on their heads, but in adopting this posture, Lilien replaces the jar with a bundle of sheaves.

11. For more on Ze'ev Raban, see Batsheva Goldman Ida, *Ze'ev Raban: A Hebrew Symbolist* (Tel Aviv: Tel Aviv Museum of Art and Yad Yzhak Ben-Zvi, 2001); Dalia Manor, "Biblical Zionism in Bezalel Art," *Israel Studies* 6, no. 1 (2001): 55–75; Gideon Ofrat, *On the Ground: Early Eretz-Israeli Art; Founding Fathers* (Jerusalem: Yaron Golan, 1993), 297–343 (in Hebrew).

12. Raban's devotion to the cause of Zionist pioneer women is evident in a poster he sketched in the late 1920s (see illustration no. 162 in *Ze'ev Raban: A Hebrew Symbolist*, 124). The poster was meant to urge Jewish women in the diaspora to donate their "jewels" (*kishutim*) to better the lives of their "pioneer sisters" in the Land of Israel. With this financial help, the women pioneers would be able to buy food and eat more than the "few olives" that they currently lived on. The poster consists of two contrasting images—one of the *halutza* who toils in agricultural work, immersed in "building the homeland," and the other of a woman who leads a luxurious life abroad, exemplified by her expensive clothing and the ballroom dancing that appears in the background. In his illustration of Ruth in the fields, however, Raban decorates his woman pioneer with the finest jewels. His princess-pioneer seems to enjoy the best of both worlds.

13. Raban used the King James Version.

14. For an extensive consideration of Raban's visual renditions of the Song of Songs, see Pardes, *Agnon's Moonstruck Lovers*, 39–41.

15. Ya'acov Ben-Dov was also the first Zionist filmmaker. For a documentary film on Ben-Dov's work, see *Ya'acov Ben-Dov: Father of the Hebrew Film*, Steven Spielberg Jewish Film Archive, 1993, https://www.youtube.com/watch?v=MW39l9LTOic (Hebrew; accessed October 28, 2021).

16. These photographs of the American Colony team are available online. See "For Shavuot: Book of Ruth Recreated 100 Years Ago," *Arutz Sheva*, June 1, 2014, at https://www.israelnationalnews .com/News/News.aspx/181273. For more on nineteenth-century Holy Land photography, see Yeshayahu Nir, *The Bible and the Image: The History of Photography in the Holy Land, 1839–1899* (Philadelphia: University of Pennsylvania Press, 1985).

17. Note that Ben-Dov also produced photographs of women pioneers in the fields. Those photos, too, were staged. The women were dressed in white for the occasion and held agricultural tools in different poses.

18. In Boris Schatz's *The New Jerusalem: The Rebuilt Reality* (Jerusalem: Bezalel Academy, 1924) (in Hebrew), this concept of Bezalel as a modern temple of sorts is developed in detail. In Raban's illustration for the title page, Schatz is seen at the Bezalel temple as he converses with his biblical precursor Bezalel Ben-Uri, the artist who was in charge of the construction of the Tabernacle.

19. In imagining a Jewish renaissance in the Land of Israel, Mapu actually relies on a mixture of the book of Ruth and the Song of Songs. He can easily blend the two texts, for in both, women loom large, and in both one finds romantic episodes within pastoral settings.

20. Fichman, "Ruth," in *Ancient Figures* (Jerusalem: Mosad Bialik, 1948), 19–50 (in Hebrew) (translation mine). Fichman also wrote an essay on the book of Ruth titled "Three Essays" (*shalosh reshimot*), in Fichman, *Selected Writings (Asif)* (Tel Aviv: Masada, 1959), 133–137. There his debt to Goethe's reading of the book of Ruth as idyllic is made explicit. For more on Fichman's "Ruth," see Ruth Kartun-Blum, "Between Versions: On Yaacov Fichman's 'Ruth,'" *Moznaim* 32 (March–April 1971): 320–329.

21. The Second Aliyah was a highly influential wave of immigration between 1904 and 1914, during which approximately forty thousand Jews, primarily from eastern Europe, immigrated to Palestine.

22. For more on Agnon's biography, see Benjamin Harshav, Introduction to *Only Yesterday*, trans. Barbara Harshav (Princeton: Princeton University Press, 2000), vii–xxix; Alan L. Mintz and Anne Golomb Hoffman, "Agnon as Modernist: The Contours of a Career," introduction to *A Book That Was Lost: Thirty-Five Stories* (expanded edition), ed. Alan Mintz and Anne Golomb Hoffman (New Milford, Conn: Toby Press, 2008), 9–34.

23. S. Y. Agnon, *Only Yesterday*, trans. Barbara Harshav, 159.

24. The first to notice the stamp of Ruth in this novella was

Eliezer Schweid in a brief essay titled "In the Path of Repentance: Agnon's *In the Prime of Her Life*," in *Three Generations of Hebrew Literature* (Tel Aviv: Am Oved, 1964), 62–70 (in Hebrew). For an extensive reading of Agnon's rereading of Ruth in "In the Prime of Her Life," see Ilana Pardes, "Gleaning in Alien Fields: Agnon, Ruth, and the Question of Estrangement," in *Literature as a Cultural Heroine*, ed. Orr Scharf (Tel Aviv: Schocken, 2021) (in Hebrew), 152–165.

25. The name of the town is not mentioned explicitly, but the characters of this novella—Tirtza and Mazal—appear in "Simple Story" as part of the Jewish life in Shibush. See Shemuel Werses, *Agnon Literally* (Jerusalem: Bialik Institute, 2000), 45–46 (in Hebrew).

26. Agnon's choice to have Tirtza write in biblical Hebrew is culturally specific. Jewish women from the Enlightenment on could study Bible and biblical Hebrew but were not exposed to rabbinic literature. See Iris Parush, *Reading Jewish Women: Marginality and Modernization in Nineteenth-Century Eastern European Jewish Society* (Waltham, Mass.: Brandeis University Press, 2004). Tirtza's Hebrew style is reminiscent of that of Mapu.

27. The recording of Agnon's reading of the opening of *In the Prime of her Life* is available online: https://www.youtube.com/watch?v=2zgFZ6622Ho (accessed October 28, 2021).

28. S. Y. Agnon, *In the Prime of Her Life*, in *8 Great Hebrew Short Novels*, trans. Gabriel Levin, ed. Alan Lelchuk and Gershon Shaked (New Milford, Conn.: Toby Press, 2005), 189. All citations are from this translation.

29. For more on Tirtza's merging with her mother, see Ariel Hirschfeld, *Reading S. Y. Agnon* (Tel Aviv: Ahuzat Bayit, 2011), 91–103 (in Hebrew).

30. Interestingly, Mazal too sets out to realize his mother's unfulfilled dreams. His mother (another Ruth-like figure in the novella) was a convert. While adopting the Jewish faith, she did not manage to become part of the Jewish people. In moving from Vienna to Shibush and joining its Jewish community, Mazal, as he admits openly, strives to redress this lack in his mother's life.

31. The quest for reparation and its discontents is a major theme in Agnon's work. For more on this topic, see Baruch Kurzweil, *Essays on S. Y. Agnon* (Tel Aviv: Schocken, 1970) (in Hebrew); Galili Shachar, *Bodies and Names: Readings in Modern Jewish Literature* (Tel Aviv: Am Oved, 2016), 137–149 (in Hebrew).

32. On Agnon's debt to Freud, see Arnold Band, "Agnon Discovers Freud's Face," in Band, *Profound Questions* (Beersheba: Dvir/Heksherim, University of Ben-Gurion, 2007), 207–218 (in Hebrew). For a consideration of the relevance of Freud to *In the Prime of Her Life*, see Nitza Ben-Dov, *Unhappy Loves: Erotic Frustration, Art and Death in the Works of Agnon* (Tel Aviv: Am Oved, 1997) (in Hebrew); Pardes, "Gleaning in Alien Fields."

33. All quotations from *In the Prime of Her Life* are on page 244.

34. For more on the intertwined individual and collective loves in Agnon's *Betrothed* and "Edo and Enam," see Pardes, *Agnon's Mooonstruck Lovers.*

35. Agnon was well aware of the Zoharic readings of the book of Ruth. In fact, in Agnon's anthology *Book, Writer, Story*, he cites a few passages from the Zohar on Ruth. In more subtle ways, Agnon intimates that there are more similarities between Zionist exegetes and Zoharic ones than might appear. Although Zionism presented itself as a decisive break with diasporic Jewish traditions, ironically, its quest to repair the exilic condition bears a curious resemblance to the Kabbalistic quest for the tikkun of the uprooted Shekhinah. In both cases, repair seems to be more of a passionate dream than a remedy for the dislocations of the world.

36. Note that Tirtza could have married the Zionist Landau (whose name means "land"), but she chooses instead to pursue the older, diasporic Akavia Mazal.

37. Shapira, "The Bible and Israeli Identity," 34–36.

38. Julia Kristeva, *Strangers to Ourselves*, trans. Leon S. Roudiez (New York: Columbia University Press, 1991), 75.

39. Bonnie Honig, "Ruth, the Model Emigrée: Mourning and the Symbolic Politics of Immigration," *Political Theory* 25, no. 1 (1997): 112–136.

40. To mention but a few more books from the 1980s and 1990s that provide feminist readings of the book of Ruth: Mieke Bal, *Leathal Love* (1987); Ilana Pardes, *Countertraditions in the Bible* (1992); and Athalya Idan-Brenner, ed., *Feminist Companion to the Bible: Ruth* (1993).

41. For more on Ben-Naftali's *Chronicle of Separation*, see Timothy Duffy's review in *Ariel* 47, no. 4 (October 2016): 194–197.

42. Michal Ben-Naftali, *Chronicle of Separation: On Deconstruction's Disillusioned Love*, trans. Mirjam Hadar (New York: Fordham University Press, 2015), 146. All future citations are from this translation.

43. Ibid., 147.

44. Ibid., 156.

45. Kristeva, *Strangers to Ourselves*, 1.

46. For more on Nes's *Biblical Stories* series, see Susan Chevlowe, *Adi Nes* (Tel Aviv: Tel Aviv Museum of Art, 2007), 126–116; *Adi Nes Biblical Stories*, Wexner Center for the Arts, Ohio State University, February 2–April 13, 2008, http://www.adines.com/content/wexner_center_for_the_arts_brochure.htm.

47. The choice to leave the staged photographs untitled is a common feature of Nes's series.

48. Adi Nes produced another, less-known staged photograph of Ruth and Naomi in a deserted storage house that is not modeled on Millet's painting.

49. For more on Agnès Varda's *The Gleaners and I*, see Homay King, "Matter, Time, and the Digital: Varda's *The Gleaners and I*," *Quarterly Review of Film and Video* 24 (2007): 421–429; Virginia Bonner, "The Gleaners and 'Us': The Radical Modesty of Agnès Varda's *Les glaneurs et la glaneuse*," in *Documenting the Documentary: Close Readings of Documentary Films and Video*, ed. Barry Keith Grant and Jeannette Sloniowski (Detroit: Wayne State University Press, 2014), 494–506.

50. *Adi Nes Biblical Stories*. Interview with Adi Nes, May 17, 2015, Beit Avihai (in Hebrew): https://www.bac.org.il/blog/?postID=12895.

51. It is noteworthy that in 1989 Ruth Calderon co-established

Elul, the first beit midrash in which secular and religious women and men studied and taught together. The success of the Jerusalemite Elul led her, a few years later, to found ALMA in Tel Aviv.

52. See the poster of the 2014 ALMA event at http://www .alma.org.il/newsletter.asp?id=243 and the program of the 2018 event at Shittim Institute at https://rashut-harabim.org/%D7%AA %D7%99%D7%A7%D7%95%D7%A0%D7%99-% D7%9C%D7%99%D7%9C-%D7%A9%D7%91%D7%95%D7 %A2%D7%95%D7%AA-%D7%A0%D7%91%D7%97%D7% A8%D7%99%D7%9D-%D7%9E%D7%A8%D7 %97%D7%91%D7%99-%D7%94%D7%90%D7% A8%D7%A5 (in Hebrew)

53. Joseph Cedar was influenced by Agnon's perspective on scholars—primarily by tales such as "Forevermore" (*ad olam*) and the novel *Shira*. For more on the book of Ruth in contemporary Israeli culture, see Galia Vachman, *Ruth: A New Israeli Commentary* (Jerusalem: Avi Hai, 2018).

Chapter 6. The American Outcast

1. Emma Lazarus, "The New Colossus": www.poetryfounda tion.org/poems/46550/the-new-colossus. Emma Lazarus (1849–1887) was born in New York into a large Sephardic Jewish family. She was the first successful Jewish poet in the United States and a friend of leading poets such as Emerson. In addition to her literary work, Lazarus was an activist on behalf of poor Jewish immigrants from eastern Europe. See Esther Schor's biography, *Emma Lazarus* (New York: Schocken, 2006).

2. The story of the composition of "Kaddish" begins on the preceding night. Ginsberg was up all night with his friend Zev Putterman, who lived on the other side of town. They listened to Ray Charles albums and read Shelley's "Adonais" while taking drugs. In the early hours of the morning, Allen asked Putterman to read him the Kaddish from his old Bar Mitzva book. When Ginsberg stepped outdoors, with the rhythms of the Kaddish, "Adonais," and Ray Charles mingling in his head, he had a vision of his mother walking down the same streets fifty years earlier. On the

writing of "Kaddish," see Ginsberg, "How Kaddish Happened," and Bill Morgan, "Some Words on Allen Ginsberg's Kaddish," in the extended fiftieth-anniversary edition of Ginsberg, *Kaddish and Other Poems, 1958–1960* (San Francisco: City Lights, 2010).

3. For more on the Lower East Side as a symbol of Jewish experience, see Hasia R. Diner, *Lower East Side Memories: A Jewish Place in America* (Princeton: Princeton University Press, 2000).

4. For more on Naomi Ginsberg's life, see Bill Morgan, *I Celebrate Myself: The Somewhat Private Life of Allen Ginsberg* (New York: Penguin, 2006).

5. Ginsberg, "Howl," in *Howl and Other Poems* (San Francisco: City Lights, 1956, 1959), 9.

6. Ginsberg, "Kaddish," in *Kaddish and Other Poems, 1958–1960*. All future citations are from this edition and will appear parenthetically within the text.

7. See Morgan, "Some Words on Allen Ginsberg's Kaddish," 103–104.

8. For more on the role of the Kaddish in Jewish American literature, see Hana Wirth-Nesher, *Call It English: The Languages of Jewish American Literature* (Princeton: Princeton University Press, 2006), 161–176.

9. Hana Wirth-Nesher, "Traces of the Past: Multilingual Jewish American Writing," in *A Cambridge Companion to Jewish American Literature*, ed. Michael P. Kramer and Hana Wirth-Nesher (Cambridge: Cambridge University Press, 2003), 114. On the hyphenated identities of American Jewry, see Arnold Eisen, "Choosing Chosenness in America: The Changing Faces of Judaism," in *Immigration and Religion in America: Comparative and Historical Perspectives*, ed. Richard Alba, Albert J. Raboteau, and Josh DeWind (New York: New York University Press, 2009), 224–245.

10. On Ginsberg's debt to other religions, see Yaakov Ariel, "From a Jewish Communist to a Jewish Buddhist: Allen Ginsberg as a Forerunner of a New American Jew," *Religions* 10, no. 2 (2019): 100, doi:10.3390/rel10020100.

11. In the course of the Great Migration almost six million African Americans moved from the South to the North. It was a

phenomenon that changed the face of America between 1915 and 1970. For more on the Great Migration, see Milton Sernett, *Bound for the Promised Land: African Americans' Religion and the Great Migration* (Durham, N.C.: Duke University Press, 1997); Isabel Wilkerson, *The Warmth of Other Suns: The Epic Story of America's Great Migration* (New York: Vintage, 2010).

12. Indebted to the great resonance of the King James Bible in African American literature (from slave spirituals to the novels of Zora Neal Hurston and James Baldwin), Morrison chooses to adhere to the title of the King James translation—Song of Solomon—rather than to the more accurate translation of *shir ha-shirim*: Song of Songs.

13. Albert Raboteau provides an extensive consideration of the changing meanings of the story of the Exodus in African American culture in "African-Americans, Exodus, and the American Israel," in *African-American Christianity: Essays in History*, ed. Paul E. Johnson (Berkeley: University of California Press, 1994), 1–17.

14. Interestingly, Morrison and Phyllis Trible discovered the feminist potentiality of the book of Ruth at roughly the same time; Trible's *God and the Rhetoric of Sexuality* was published in 1978.

15. Toni Morrison, *Song of Solomon* (New York: Signet, 1977), 125. All future citations are from this edition and will be given parenthetically in the text.

16. For a reading of this scene in *Song of Solomon* in relation to the threshing floor episode, see Beth Benedrix, "Intimate Fatality: *Song of Solomon* and the Journey Home," in *Toni Morrison and the Bible: Contested Intertextualities*, ed. Shirley A. Stave (New York: Peter Lang, International Academic Publishers, 2006), 110.

17. Morrison offers another fascinating mixture of the book of Ruth and the Song of Songs in *Beloved*. The stamp of the Song is evident in the different variations on the verse "I am my Beloved's and he is mine" in the polyphonic song of Sethe and her two daughters at the end of the novel. But given that this song revolves around the love of a mother and her daughters, it is also indebted to the book of Ruth. Above all, it is the recurrent line "I will never leave you again" that calls to mind Ruth's oath on the road. For more on

Morrison's renditions of the Song of Songs in *Song of Solomon* and *Beloved*, see Ilana Pardes, *The Song of Songs: A Biography*, 198–216.

18. Quoted in Therese E. Higgins, *Religiosity, Cosmology, and Folklore: The African Influence in the Novels of Toni Morrison* (New York: Routledge, 2001), 5.

19. *Drums and Shadows: Survival Studies Among the Georgia Coastal Negroes*, Savannah Unit, Georgia Writers' Project (Athens: University of Georgia Press, 1940). The African tales and songs of *Drums and Shadows* were collected in the 1930s. On Morrison's use of *Drums and Shadows*, see Higgins, *Religiosity, Cosmology, and Folklore*, 5–28. For more on the major role of oral culture in *Song of Solomon*, see Joyce Irene Middleton, "From Orality to Literacy: Oral Memory in Toni Morrison's *Song of Solomon*," in *New Essays on Song of Solomon*, ed. Valerie Smith (Cambridge: Cambridge University Press, 1995), 19–40.

20. Quoted in Higgins, *Religiosity, Cosmology, and Folklore*, 9.

21. Albert J. Raboteau, *Slave Religion: The "Invisible Institution" in the Antebellum South* (Oxford: Oxford University Press), 243–266.

22. For more on the maternal legacy in the novel, see Marianne Hirsch, "Knowing Their Names: Toni Morrison's *Song of Solomon*," in *New Essays on Song of Solomon*, ed. Valerie Smith (Cambridge: Cambridge University Press, 1995), 69–92.

23. To be more precise, del Toro is a rather mobile immigrant—he primarily lives in Los Angeles but spends a few months every year both in Mexico and in Toronto.

24. Del Toro's speech is available on YouTube: https://www.youtube.com/watch?v=n_f-ofpai18.

25. A transcript and video of the interview is available at the Charlie Rose website: "A Conversation with Guillermo del Toro," July 2, 2009, http://charlierose.com/videos/14026.

26. Henry Koster was born Hermann Kosterlitz in Berlin to Jewish parents. He was introduced to cinema in 1910 when his uncle opened a movie theater in Berlin. Koster became a film director but had to flee Germany due to the rise of antisemitism in the early 1930s. In 1936, after several years in France, Koster was

signed to a contract with Universal and brought to Hollywood
with several other refugees, among them Joe Pasternak, who later
became an influential film producer. He stayed at Universal until
1941, then worked for MGM, and around 1948 moved over to 20th
Century–Fox. Koster made numerous films—primarily musicals
and family dramas. He was nominated for an Academy Award for
The Bishop's Wife (1947).

27. On Hollywood's biblical projects, see *Semeia* 74 (1996),
special issue: "Biblical Glamour and Hollywood Glitz." See also
the collected essays on one of Hollywood's most influential biblical epics, *Ben-Hur*, in Barbara Ryan and Milette Shamir, eds., *Big-
ger Than Ben-Hur: The Novel, Its Adaptations, and Their Audiences*
(Syracuse, N.Y.: Syracuse University Press, 2015).

28. Quoted in George Macdonald Fraser, *The Hollywood History of the World* (London: Penguin, 1988), xii.

29. *The Story of Ruth* has been available on YouTube since 2012
and has been viewed by numerous viewers on the internet.

30. On the interpretive choices of Koster's adaptation of Ruth,
see J. Cheryl Exum, "Is This Naomi?" in Exum, *Plotted, Shot, and
Painted: Cultural Representations of Biblical Women* (Sheffield, UK:
Sheffield Phoenix University Press, 2012), 161–208.

31. For more on the multiple Ruths of *The Shape of Water*, see
Jonathan Lyonhart and Jennifer Matheny, "The Monstrous Other
and the Biblical Narrative of Ruth," *Journal of Religion and Film* 24,
no. 2 (2020): article 3, doi: 10.32873/uno.dc.jrf.24.2.003.

32. Gilles Deleuze and Félix Guattari, *Kafka: Toward A Minor
Literature* (Minneapolis: University of Minnesota Press, 1986).

33. Note that del Toro does insert something of the Catholic
heritage of the Hispanic community in choosing to fashion a god-
like fish. "It's not exactly a secret that a fish is a Christian symbol,"
del Toro admits mischievously in an NPR interview: "Guillermo del
Toro Says 'Shape of Water' Is an Antidote for Today's Cynicism,"
December 1, 2017, NPR, https://www.npr.org/transcripts/567265511
(accessed October 29, 2021).

34. Del Toro bolsters the feminist dimension of the film by
choosing two actresses who had previously starred in movies that

address the struggle of marginalized women to stand for their rights—Sally Hawkins in *Maudie* (2016) and Octavia Spencer in *Hidden Figures* (2016).

35. See Angela Williams's interview with del Toro: "Guillermo del Toro Says New Movie Is 'a Fairy Tale for Troubled Times,'" December 13, 2017, ABC News, https://abcnews.go.com/Enter tainment/guillermo-del-toro-movie-fairy-tale-troubled-times /story?id=51769703 (accessed October 29, 2021).

Epilogue

1. The term *gleaner* derives from Late Latin *glennare*, of Celtic origin. Note that in Hebrew there is a similar use of the term for gleaning in literal and figurative contexts. Thus *leket* can refer both to gleaning in the fields and to a collection of commentaries or articles.

2. American and Israeli congregations have had an impact on each other. The rise of the new tikkunim in Israeli culture was indebted to American trends. And yet once the custom became a full-fledged cultural phenomenon in Israel, some of the Israeli features of the tikkunim seeped into the Jewish American sphere. Note that Ruth Calderon spent three years (2002–2005) in New York and during her stay organized events of Tikkun Leil Shavuot both at the Manhattan Jewish Community Center and at the 92nd Street Y.

3. The website of Women of Reform Judaism on Shavuot can be found at wrj.org.

4. Rabbi Rachel Grant Meyer, "What Shavuot Teaches Us About Welcoming the Stranger," June 9, 2016, HIAS: https://www .hias.org/blog/what-shavuot-teaches-us-about-welcoming-stranger.

5. Rachel Wharton, "Meet the Gleaners," *New York Times*, July 6, 2020, available at https://www.nytimes.com/2020/07/06 /dining/gleaners-farm-food-waste.html.

6. Ruth Rabbah, 2:10 (translation mine). This midrashic commentary uses the term *va-tisha'er* in the biblical text—"was left"—as its point of departure. The biblical verse goes as follows: "and the woman was left of her two children and husband" (Ruth 1:5).

7. John Keats, "Ode to a Nightingale," is available online at https://www.poetryfoundation.org/poems/44479/ode-to-a-night ingale. Benedict Cumberbatch's reading of the ode on YouTube is superb: https://www.youtube.com/watch?v=TdphtMWjies. For more on Keats's nightingale, see Helen Vendler, *The Odes of John Keats* (Cambridge, Mass: Belknap, 1983).

8. On Ruth's capacity to provide a more humanly satisfying song in "Ode to a Nightingale," see Jeffrey Baker, "Nightingale and Melancholy," in *Modern Critical Views: John Keats*, rev. ed., ed. Harold Bloom (New York: Chelsea House, 1985), 54.

9. It is noteworthy that Ginsberg had Keats on his mind when he wrote "Kaddish." He read Percy Bysshe Shelley's poem "Adonais: Elegy on the Death of John Keats" on the night preceding its composition. What is more, Ginsberg evokes Shelley's elegy in the opening lines of his own elegy on the death of his mother. Morrison, we may assume, is familiar with Keats's well-known ode, but her debt is more minimal.

ACKNOWLEDGMENTS

I HAD THE GOOD FORTUNE of having many conversations with Ruth aficionados while writing this book. I am grateful to Robert Alter, Amir Eshel, and Steve Weitzman for reading the entire manuscript and offering valuable suggestions. I also benefited from an ongoing Zoom hevruta with Leora Batnitzky and Vivian Liska, my dear fellow travelers, and am deeply indebted to their thoughtful responses. Given the broad scope of the book, I had the pleasure of consulting other friends and colleagues, from a variety of research fields, who offered vital insights at different stations along the way: Jonatan Benarroch, Michal Ben-Naftali, Ruth Calderon, Richard Cohen, Noam Gal, Ruth HaCohen, Galit Hasan-Rokem, Melila Hellner-Eshed, Ariel Hirschfeld, Moshe Idel, Ruth Kara-Ivanov Kaniel, Yehuda Liebes, Daniel Matt, Naphtali Meshel, Benjamin Porat, Yosefa Raz, Sarit Shalev-Eyni, Milette Shamir, Gal Ventura, and Haim Weiss.

I am grateful to the astute students of several seminars I gave on the book of Ruth at the Hebrew University of Jerusalem. I pre-

ACKNOWLEDGMENTS

sented different portions of the book at the Hebrew University, the University of California, Berkeley, Princeton University, and Stanford University and am grateful for the response of the audiences on these occasions. Many thanks go to my gifted research assistants Miri Avissar and Shira Mazuz for their ongoing help.

David Lobenstine was as insightful as always. I cherish his remarkable editorial work and am grateful for his encouragement to continue gleaning even at moments in which I thought I had already said all that I possibly could. I am grateful to the Israel Science Foundation for financial support (1707/15).

I am greatly indebted to Steven J. Zipperstein for inviting me to write a biography of Ruth for the Jewish Lives series and for his generous support throughout. Many thanks go to the editorial team at Yale University Press. I am grateful to Heather Gold, associate editor, for her assistance. I have been fortunate to have Susan Laity as my manuscript editor. I owe much to her masterful and meticulous comments and suggestions.

The book of Ruth is among other things a book about familial bonds. My family—Itamar, Eyal, and Keren—have been an incredible source of love and encouragement.

This book is dedicated to my beloved children Keren and Eyal. Going with them wherever they go has been one of the greatest pleasures of my life.

Thirty-six lines of "Kaddish" from *Collected Poems 1947–1997*, Allen Ginsberg. Copyright © 2006 by the Allen Ginsberg Trust, used by permission of HarperCollins Publishers.

Excerpts from "Kaddish" by Allen Ginsberg, currently collected in *Collected Poems 1947–1997*. Copyright © 1961, 2006 Allen Ginsberg, LLC, used by permission of The Wylie Agency (UK) Limited.

INDEX

Bible (*continued*)
on, during the Enlightenment,
95–96; as oriental gem, 103–105;
scholarly methodologies applied
to, 96. *See also* Ruth, book of
Bible de Tours, Doré's illustrations for,
107
Boaz: and courtship of Ruth, 21–26;,
181n24; in Doré's art, 108; in
European pastoral art, 88–92,
94–95; genealogy of, 39–40; as
go'el, 29–30, 31, 33–34; and invitation to Ruth to join the harvesters' meal, 60, 97; and the law
of redemption, 34–35; in Millet's
paintings, 97; as Obed's father,
40; in Poussin's *Summer*, 90–91;
rival to, 31, 33–34; Ruth's marriage
to, 3, 33–36; Ruth's seduction of,
26–32, 54–58, 133; and Ruth the
Shekhinah, 69–71, 77, 79; in the
Zohar, 69–71, 77, 79
Boyarin, Daniel, 55
Bruriah, 46
Buber, Martin, 4, 116–117

Calderon, Ruth, 140
Carolsfeld, Julius Schnorr von, *Ruth in
Boaz's Field*, 94–95, 105
Cedar, Joseph, *Footnote*, 141
Ceres, 92
Chilion, 35, 40; migration of, 1–2
Christ, as Messiah, 61
Christianity, rise of, 43
conversion, William James's definition
of, 50
conversion to Judaism: approaches to,
43–45; Babylonian Talmud on,
50–51; laws of, 43, 48, 50–52
converts, embrace of, 43–44. *See also*
Ruth—as convert
Creature from the Black Lagoon (film),
160, 162

David, King, 5, 6, 39; in the Midrash,
79; as portrayed in the *Midrash
Ha-Ne'lam*, 71–73; Ruth as fore-

mother of, 3, 40, 58–61, 70, 76,
78; in Zionist culture, 120; in the
Zohar, 72–73, 76, 78
deconstruction, as applied to interpretation of Ruth's story, 131
Deleuze, Gilles, 163
del Toro, Guillermo, 144–145; background of, 159; as an immigrant,
159; and monsters as analogous
to immigrants, 162–163. See also
Shape of Water
Demeter, 85, 92
DeMille, Cecil B., *The Ten Commandments*, 160–161
Deuteronomy, book of, 20, 25, 34, 43,
53, 63, 141, 144
Doré, Gustave: Bible illustrations by,
107–110; *Ruth in the Field*, 109
*Drums and Shadows: Survival Studies
Among the Georgia Coastal
Negroes*, 157

Ecclesiastes, 40, 78, 126
Eglon, 2, 118
Eliezer, Tobiah ben, *Lekach Tov*, 62
Elimelech, 24, 34, 35; migration of, 1–2
Eliot, George, *Middlemarch*, 5
Er, 36
Exodus, book of, 29, 62
Ezekiel, book of, 30
Ezra, 6

Fichman, Jacob, "Ruth," 123
Frank, Jacob, 74

Gandhi, Mahatma, 4
Gautier, Théophile, 101
Genesis, book of, 20, 23, 27, 36–37, 75,
77, 102
ger, 22; as convert, 43; as foreign resident, 42
German biblical criticism, 103–104
Ginsberg, Allen, 144–45; "Howl," 146;
"Kaddish (For Naomi Ginsberg,
1894–1956)," 145, 146–152, 168,
199n2, 205n9; as Ruth, in his devotion to his mother, 147–152, 173

Solomon: The Lure of Wisdom, by Steven Weitzman
Steven Spielberg: A Life in Films, by Molly Haskell
Alfred Stieglitz: Taking Pictures, Making Painters, by Phyllis Rose
Barbra Streisand: Redefining Beauty, Femininity, and Power,
      by Neal Gabler
Leon Trotsky: A Revolutionary's Life, by Joshua Rubenstein
Warner Bros: The Making of an American Movie Studio,
      by David Thomson

FORTHCOMING TITLES INCLUDE:

Abraham, by Anthony Julius
Hannah Arendt, by Masha Gessen
Franz Boas, by Noga Arikha
Mel Brooks, by Jeremy Dauber
Alfred Dreyfus, by Maurice Samuels
Anne Frank, by Ruth Franklin
Betty Friedan, by Rachel Shteir
George Gershwin, by Gary Giddins
Allen Ginsberg, by Ed Hirsch
Herod, by Martin Goodman
Jesus, by Jack Miles
Josephus, by Daniel Boyarin
Louis Kahn, by Gini Alhadeff
Mordecai Kaplan, by Jenna Weissman Joselit
Carole King, by Jane Eisner
Fiorello La Guardia, by Brenda Wineapple
Mahler, by Leon Botstein
Norman Mailer, by David Bromwich
Maimonides, by Alberto Manguel
Louis B. Mayer and Irving Thalberg, by Kenneth Turan
Golda Meir, by Deborah E. Lipstadt